Working with Children in Groups

A Handbook for Counsellors, Educators and Community Workers

KATHRYN GELDARD

and

DAVID GELDARD

palgrave

22428909

First published 2001 by
PALGRAVE
Houndmills, Basingstoke, Hampshire RG21 6XS and
175 Fifth Avenue, New York, N.Y. 10010
Companies and representatives throughout the world

PALGRAVE is the new global academic imprint of St. Martin's Press LLC Scholarly and Reference Division and Palgrave Publishers Ltd (formerly Macmillan Press Ltd).

ISBN 0–333–92143–7

This book is printed on paper suitable for recycling and made from fully managed and sustained forest sources.

A catalogue record for this book is available from the British Library.

10   9   8   7   6   5   4   3   2
10   09   08   07   06   05   04   03

Printed and bound in Great Britain by
Antony Rowe Ltd, Chippenham and Eastbourne

Contents

List of figures and tables

Introduction

As authors, we wonder whether readers might be interested in knowing something of our backgrounds and the reason why we undertook to write this book. We decided to write the book after we ran workshops to train people from the helping professions who were interested in running groups for children. Participants at our workshops became enthusiastic about the possible beneficial outcomes of running groups for children and encouraged us to incorporate ideas generated from the workshops into a book.

Our own backgrounds have been helpful to us, when working with children in groups, in enabling us to make use of conceptual ideas and practice methods from the three professional disciplines of occupational therapy, counselling and psychology. Kathryn is an occupational therapist who has a Masters degree in counselling. David is a counselling psychologist with a strong interest in the experiential therapies such as Gestalt therapy. Kathryn spent many years as an occupational therapist working in psychiatric settings with children and young people (initially at the Johns Hopkins University Hospital in the USA, then at the Mater Children's Hospital, Brisbane, and later at the Child and Youth Mental Health Service, in Maroochydore, Australia). While doing this work she was able to compare the relative effectiveness of working with children individually with that of working with children in groups. David, as a counselling psychologist, has had extensive experience in group work as a trainer in Gestalt therapy. He has specialised in working with children, young people and their families, and was for some years the coordinator of a family therapy unit at a crisis counselling centre, Lifeline, in Brisbane, Australia.

Later, we both worked for an agency (the Talera Centre) that specialised in working with children and young people who had been exposed to violence in their families. During this time we became excited by the way in which groups for children and teenagers were powerful in helping these youngsters to change, feel better and learn more adaptive behaviours.

We have subsequently specialised, as private practitioners, in working both individually and in groups with children and young people with psychosocial problems.

We remember what it was like for us when we first started to run groups. As with many workers, we felt enthusiastic but also somewhat apprehensive and found there was a lack of practical down-to-earth information we could use as a guide. Our hope is that this book will fill that gap we experienced by providing useful information to those who read it.

KATHRYN GELDARD
DAVID GELDARD

PART I

GROUPS FOR CHILDREN

1 Why run groups?

Over a long period of time groups for children have been successfully run to fulfil a variety of purposes. Perhaps the most common example of the use of groups for children is in schools, where children are grouped together in ways which are intended to maximise their opportunities for learning. For many years community and religious organisations have run children's groups for particular purposes. In the past, many of these groups were intended to be character building. They were also used to help children learn particular social or religious beliefs and values, to help them develop social skills by interacting with other children and to develop and strengthen particular personal qualities.

In today's society, there are many different types of groups for children run by a wide range of organisations. Community, religious, government and private organisations and agencies commonly run children's groups. Groups for children are often established in schools, hospitals, mental health services and residential facilities. In recent times groups for children have been used successfully in many different settings to help children deal with emotional, behavioural, social, mental health and developmental problems.

In this book the emphasis will be primarily on groups designed to prevent dysfunctional or maladaptive behaviour, to promote personal growth and to facilitate emotional or behavioural change.

ADVANTAGES OF GROUP WORK

Before planning to run a particular children's group, a decision needs to be made whether running a group for the children concerned will be more appropriate than working individually with each child. It needs to be recognised that some children are best helped individually whereas others will benefit more by participating in a group programme.

When working individually with children a significant relationship inevitably develops between the child and the worker. Although such a relationship is helpful for children who can cope with a degree of intimacy with an adult, other children may act out, much as they would in other close relationships. For such children group work may be the best option as it diffuses the intensity of the relationship with the worker. Strong relationships do develop in a group, but for many children these tend to be directed more to peers than to the leaders (Swanson, 1996).

Some parents worry about their child entering into a one-to-one relationship with an adult in a situation where they are not present themselves. In these cases the parents' anxiety is likely to be an obstacle to effective outcomes. A similar level of parental anxiety is less likely to occur in a group situation.

When deciding whether or not to use group work, the personalities of the children concerned, the nature of their problems, and their own and their family's preferences need to be taken into account. Additionally, where there are mental health problems, consideration may need to be given to the provision of medication to enable some children to benefit from a group intervention.

When making a decision about whether to work with children individually or in a group, leaders need to be aware of the advantages of group work, and must have a conviction that group work can be used to foster healthy development and become a catalyst for growth (Kymissis, 1996).

Advantages of group work include:

1. Groups can promote change.
2. A group can parallel the wider social environment.
3. A group provides a sense of belonging.
4. Common needs can be addressed in a group.
5. Groups are cost effective.

Groups can promote change

Rose and Edleson (1987) draw attention to the power of children's groups in promoting change in individual group members. They point out that children do much of their learning by interacting with, observing and listening to peers. They believe that peer reinforcement is often more powerful than adult reinforcement and can be achieved in groups. Additionally they point out that a group can provide a child with a major source of feedback about behaviours that are annoying or pleasing to other children, and about those cognitions that appear to others to be self-defeating or self-enhancing. Thus change is promoted and can be facilitated by skilful group leaders who provide an opportunity for children to learn skills involved in giving and receiving feedback. By providing feedback to help others, the children in a group learn strategies for helping themselves.

As well as providing an opportunity for giving and receiving feedback in a safe environment, a group setting can provide an opportunity for the sharing of emotional experiences and for experimenting with new skills and behaviours (Berkovitz, 1987a,b). Leaders can construct situations in which children have opportunity, instruction and rewards for reinforcing others in the group. As children learn to reinforce others, they are likely to be reciprocally reinforced by the other children. Consequently, relationships can be enhanced and the children may start to value each other's opinions. They may learn to deal with and tolerate differences in beliefs, attitudes and behaviours. The group can then be encouraged to generalise skills learnt in the group to their wider environment.

Often children's emotional and physical behaviours are the consequence of values, opinions, beliefs and attitudes which require modification if change is to occur. Children have limited life experience and are in a process of continuous learning. A group can provide an excellent forum for the dissemination of information which may be helpful in enabling group members to change the way they think, and consequently to change the ways they feel and behave. For example, groups can be used for the teaching of protective behaviours for children who have been emotionally, physically or sexually abused. Similarly they can be used to teach new moral values such as 'abuse is not OK' for children who have witnessed domestic violence.

A group can parallel the wider social environment

A group provides an environment which in some ways simulates the wider world in which the child lives and may have some resemblance to the natural peer group. However, in contrast to the wider environment, a group can provide a level of safety for the child. The experience of being in a safe setting provides the child with more time to experiment and process information with support and encouragement. This may enable the child to become more fully self-aware, rather than to be reactive to a hostile environment. Through increased self-awareness the child may consequently change. The child may also observe the interactions and behaviours of others in the group and change may occur through vicarious learning. Because of the experiential characteristics of groups and the power of peer interactions in them, it seems probable that children in a group may be more likely to change than they would be in a one-to-one relationship with an adult.

If we are to help children we need to remember that their social interaction is a key aspect of their developmental process. When a child's normal development has been disrupted in some way, there will often be consequences with regard to his or her social behaviour with peers. Hence, interventions that directly address the interrelationships of childhood are likely to benefit the child more broadly than interventions that do not deal with these interrelationships (Kymissis, 1996). It therefore follows that there are advantages to be gained by working with children in an environment which specifically involves social interaction. A group setting provides such an environment.

For many children the advantages to be gained from social interaction by working in a group will outweigh the benefits of working individually. Additionally, for some children it will be difficult, if not impossible, to achieve desired changes by working individually, whereas these changes may be readily achieved in a group setting. For example, it is very difficult to help children change maladaptive social behaviours or to acquire socially appropriate skills when working with them individually. Similarly, it may be difficult to help a child to gain in self-esteem when working individually because self-esteem is often dependent on a child's success or failure in interacting positively with peers. In the individual counselling situation the counsellor is unable to observe the child's interactional behaviours with peers, and the child is not able to get feedback from other children in the safety of a therapeutic setting. Additionally, the opportunity to practise appropriate social skills with peers, under the guidance of the counsellor, is not available. In contrast, a group provides an excellent environment for learning and practising useful and effective social skills, as well as for developing self-esteem. For these particular purposes groups are clearly advantageous when compared with individual work. Furthermore, there are a number of different ways (see Chapter 2) in which group work offers opportunities for preventing the development of dysfunctional or maladaptive behaviour, promoting personal growth and facilitating change; opportunities which are not available when working with a child individually.

A group provides a sense of belonging

A normal developmental need of children is to have a sense of belonging, and this is achieved by being a member of one or more groups. For many children the most important group they belong to is their family. They may also belong to a number of other groups, such as peer groups, social and sporting groups. Often children who have specific problems become socially isolated and do not feel as though they fit comfortably in the groups available to them. By working in a group rather than individually, such children can be enabled to experience a sense of belonging. This sense of belonging may help them to develop positive feelings about themselves, to address problem issues and engage in personal growth.

The sense of belonging engendered by a group can provide children with motivation to work together and to pursue common goals with the aim of achieving positive outcomes for the whole group and for individual children in it. As identified by Fiedler (1967) an event which affects one member in a group is likely to affect all members. It is therefore likely that a high level of interdependence will develop in a group. This helps to boost feelings of belonging and being needed. The resulting cohesion will influence and strengthen values through consensus. As cohesion develops, so the group will develop an energy of its own which will provide a stimulus for change and action, both within and outside the group.

A sense of belonging is very important for those children who have experienced troubling life situations or events. They may be unable to talk to others about their experience either because they do not think others could understand, or because they are ashamed or embarrassed because of their experiences. For these children a sense of belonging within a group enables them to feel less marginalised and to have an opportunity to normalise their experiences with consequent reduction of feelings of stigmatisation (LeCroy and Rose, 1986).

Common needs can be addressed

Often there are considerable advantages in working with children who have common needs in a group setting rather than an individual setting. Frequently workers in an agency, government department, hospital, clinic, school or other educational institution discover they are involved with a number of individual children who have common needs. Sometimes these children may all be clients of the workers involved. At other times they may include children in the wider community who demonstrate similar problems and/or needs. Staff members may observe that children in the neighbourhood are being, or have been, negatively affected by a common occurrence or event. For example, children may have been traumatised by a fatal shooting (Fatout, 1996). Such children have had a common experience and may have been similarly affected.

In a school setting there may be groups of children who have study problems, social skills problems, who are bullies or are being bullied, or who have difficulty in managing particular emotions or behaviours. There may also be a number of children who share a common disorder such as Attention Deficit Hyperactivity Disorder or an anxiety disorder.

In any community generally there are certain to be numbers of children who have experienced family dysfunction, family break-up, domestic violence, the problems of blended families, the loss of a significant other through death or separation or who have suffered neglect, physical or emotional abuse.

Mental health workers are faced with meeting the demands of children with a wide range of problems including those children who are suicidal, psychotic, have personality disorders, impulse control disorders, adjustment disorders and those who suffer from anxiety, stress and depression. Moreover, at the beginning of the twenty-first century in western society, workers are increasingly needing to help children who have drug and alcohol related problems.

Hospital staff are confronted with the emotional problems of children with severe disability, those who have siblings or parents who are dying, those who are disabled and those who have chronic illness.

With every type of problem described above it would be possible to address each child's needs individually, provided that the human service resources were available. By using group work so that the children's needs are addressed collectively, a larger number of children may be able to receive help simultaneously. Furthermore, the help may be more effective because of the special characteristics of group work.

In the past many workers assumed that children who are in crisis or who experienced a severe trauma, for example death of a significant other, were poor candidates for groups. This assumption was often made on the basis that such children would not receive the necessary support and guidance in a group that could be given to them in individual therapy. In recent years topic-focused groups have been widely used. A topic-focused group is a group which comprises children from a particular target group with common needs and issues (see Chapter 3). An example would be a group for children who have been traumatised by sexual abuse. Swanson (1996) points out that with the advent of topic-focused groups the needs of children who are in crisis or have experienced severe trauma can often be met in a group format. Our own experience strongly validates this belief.

Groups are cost-effective

Generally, group work is likely to be cost-effective when compared with individual work. There has been a gain in popularity in recent years of short-term group psychotherapy for young people in the mental health field where the emphasis is on briefer, less costly, treatments which can be carried out in an outpatient rather than an inpatient setting. Such treatment maximises the therapeutic gain for each group member while containing treatment costs (Dies, 1996).

Unfortunately, to date, little hard research data concerning children has been published to compare the cost-effectiveness of individual psycho-educational, counselling and therapeutic work with similar work carried out in a group setting. Research with adults does suggest that when group, instead of individual, work is used similar results can be obtained at far lower costs (Toseland and Siporin, 1986; and Teri and Lewinsohn, 1985).

LIMITATIONS OF GROUP WORK

Although there are many advantages associated with the use of group work when working with some children, it cannot be assumed that in all cases group work is necessarily the best option. Group work may be unsuitable for a variety of reasons and for particular groups of children. Certainly, working with children in a group setting would be problematic for groups of children who:

- lack impulse control and cannot control their exuberance and aggressiveness (Kraft, 1996)
- quickly display aggressive behaviour, are destructive to property, sometimes use toys and property as weapons and respond on a behavioural continuum between detachment and defiance (Gupta, Harriton and Kernberg, 1996)
- are of incompatible developmental ages
- have psychotic disorders and are likely to decompensate as a result of the stress of the social exchanges required in a group (Gupta, Harriton and Kernberg, 1996)
- have expressive or mixed receptive–expressive language disorder and may have difficulty expressing their frustration other than with aggressive outbursts (Gupta, Harriton and Kernberg, 1996).

Running groups for children who fit the descriptions in the above list is unlikely to benefit the children concerned unless these groups are specifically designed to meet well defined and limited goals. Running groups for such children is also likely to present group leaders with significant difficulties. However, it is sometimes possible to include one or two children from some of the above categories in a group where peer relationships can be used to influence behaviour.

Although group work has some advantages over approaches where children are treated individually, there are also some limitations (Dwivedi, 1993a). An important limitation of group work is that some individual children may be unable to talk openly about important personal issues in a group setting. Conversely, it is also true that some children may be unable to talk openly in a one-to-one relationship with an adult. In a group setting, however, they may be enabled to share their experiences if other children have disclosed similar experiences to theirs. For those children who are unable to share in a group it may be possible to identify their issues in a group setting and then address them in individual work later.

When working with a group, it is not feasible to spend a significant amount of time addressing the individual and personal needs of one child. Children who have high levels of emotional disturbance may need individual therapeutic work, although in some cases it can be useful to engage a child in individual work whilst concurrently participating in a group programme.

An important limitation of group work is that groups cannot be run without adequate material and human resources and these may not be available in some settings (see Chapter 4).

The generalisation of change

There may be limits to the extent to which changes achieved within a group generalise to the wider environment. Clearly a goal of group work is for the child to transfer what has been learnt in the group to life in the outside word. There is also an expectation that what has been learnt will persist after the group has finished. Unfortunately, unless particular attention is paid to the goals of generalisation and persistence, these may not be achieved. It is naive to think they will necessarily occur.

For generalisation to occur, repetition of newly learnt behaviours over a period of time is required and the children need to be provided with motivating influences such as the use of rewards and consequences that encourage use of new skills and behaviours (Adelman and Taylor, 1982). Generalisation can be enhanced through the use of homework, which is designed to give the child an opportunity to practise what has been learnt in the group. This practice is then carried out independently in a different environment and without the support of the group leader. Additionally, it can be useful to invite parents, carers and/or teachers to cooperate in helping the child to achieve the desired changes. Success or difficulty in carrying out homework and achieving a desired outcome can then be reported back to the group by the child so that his/her experience can be validated. Where outcomes are successful they should be made newsworthy.

2 Types of group

In this chapter the following types of groups for children will be discussed:

1. Therapy groups
2. Counselling groups
3. Psycho-educational groups
4. Personal growth groups
5. Support groups
6. Developmental skills groups

Each of these types of group will influence the child's development in some way, with the consequence that change of a positive nature is likely. There are many other types of groups for children. Some provide care when the parents or permanent carers are not available to do this. Others enable children to join together for particular activities, such as drama, craft work or sports. These will not be discussed, because the focus of this book is specifically on groups primarily designed to promote change in children.

Before describing the six types of group listed above, we need to consider a number of theoretical approaches that can be used by group leaders to produce change.

THEORETICAL APPROACHES FOR PRODUCING CHANGE

In order to maximise facilitating change in children, group leaders need to have a clear understanding of the theoretical approach they intend to use. There are several quite different approaches, with each approach having its own explanations of the ways in which change occurs and can be promoted. Most commonly, group leaders will use one of the following:

- A psychoanalytic approach
- An experiential therapies approach
- A post-modern approach
- A cognitive/behavioural approach
- A behaviour therapy approach
- A developmental approach

The psychoanalytic approach

The aim of the psychoanalytic approach is to make unconscious motives conscious. This may produce spontaneous change in the child. Moreover, once unconscious motives are conscious, the child can exercise choice and make changes. From this perspective a 'cure' is based on uncovering the meaning of symptoms, the causes of behaviour and the repressed materials that interfere with healthy functioning. It is to be noted however that intellectual insight alone does not resolve symptoms. The child's need to cling to old patterns must be confronted by working through transference distortions (Corey, 1996).

In a group setting, the psychoanalytic process of change occurs as a consequence of external and internal forces at work within the child which derive from the unique interactions occurring in the group. The therapist treats the group as a whole and assists the group to look for the latent themes underlying the manifest behaviour (Kraft, 1996).

Experiential approaches

Experiential approaches include Client-centred Therapy (Rogers, 1955, 1965); Gestalt Therapy (Perls, Hefferline and Goodman, 1951; Clarkson, 1989); the experiential approaches of Gendlin (1981), and Mahrer (1983), and the existential approaches of Bugental (1978) and Yalom (1980). Additionally there are the emotionally focused expressive therapies of Janov (1970) and Pierce, Nichols, and DuBrin (1983). The transpersonal approach (Hastings, 1999) also falls within this category.

Although the experiential approaches vary with regard to concepts and techniques, they nevertheless share a number of distinctive features (Rice and Greenberg, 1992). All these approaches utilise the phenomenological method, taking the client's ongoing awareness of his of her own experience as the primary datum for therapy. They define the facilitation of experiencing as the key therapeutic task (Greenberg, Elliott and Lietaer, 1994), and are thus discovery oriented. They consider an egalitarian, person-centred therapeutic relationship central to therapy, and seek to further the client's potential for growth, self-determination and choice. The experiential approaches assume that new, and/or raised, awareness and the generation of new meaning are the basis of change.

Post-modern approaches

The two most significant post-modern approaches are Solution Focused Therapy (deShazer, 1991) and Narrative Therapy (White and Epston, 1990). Central to these is the use of constructivist thinking. According to constructivist theory people form constructs which encapsulate their concepts about the world in which they live. These constructs, or personal interpretations of the world, are not fixed, but are revised and replaced as new information becomes available to the individual concerned (Kelly, 1955). This suggests that each person behaves like a scientist, formulating hypotheses to explain life's experiences. These hypotheses are then tested and revised as new experiences are encountered.

The Solution Focused Therapy model is structured around core assumptions: first, that all clients have the strength and resources to change, second, the idea that no problem happens all the time, and third, that there are exceptions to the rule (for example, someone who is anxious is not anxious all the time, and there will be times when that person is not anxious). Once exceptions are identified, the counsellor helps the client to form specific goals by using specific questioning techniques.

Narrative Therapy is based on the notion that people find meaning in their lives by organising their experiences and external events into stories, which they then incorporate into a larger life narrative. As clients tell their stories the therapist helps them both to discover that these stories are social constructions that are not fixed, and to realise that other stories may be more suitable.

Cognitive/behavioural approaches

The Cognitive Behavioural Therapies are especially useful in helping children to modify their attitudes, beliefs and constructs about life, and to change their behaviours. They stress the role of thinking, questioning, deciding, doing and re-deciding. These approaches are psycho-educational as they emphasise therapy as a learning process. The process includes acquiring and practising new skills, learning new ways of thinking and acquiring more effective ways of coping with problems (Corey, 1996).

Rational Emotive Behaviour Therapy (REBT) and Cognitive Therapy (CT) are the most commonly used of these approaches. When using REBT the therapist functions as a teacher, is highly directive and teaches clients a specific model for changing cognitions (Ellis, 1995; Dryden, 1990). This is not the case in CT where the focus is on a collaborative relationship between therapist and client. In CT the therapist assists the client to identify dysfunctional beliefs, discover alternative rules for living and then promotes corrective experiences which lead to learning new skills (Beck, 1993).

The behaviour therapy approach

Behaviour therapy focuses on current overt behaviour. Therapy is based on the principles of learning theory which assumes that behaviour is learnt through reinforcement and imitation. Maladaptive behaviour is assumed to be the consequence of faulty learning (Bandura, 1986). The therapist focuses on the factors influencing behaviour to discover ways of addressing problem behaviours. The client is encouraged to set goals, experiment with new behaviours and evaluate the extent to which goals are being met. The therapist is active and directive and functions as a teacher or trainer in helping clients learn more effective behaviour. Techniques used include shaping behaviour through the use of contracts with specific consequences for particular outcomes.

A major problem with behaviour therapy when used as the sole treatment method is that it addresses overt symptomatic behaviour while ignoring underlying emotional and psychological issues. When working with children in groups, however, behaviour therapy may be useful if used in conjunction with other approaches.

The developmental approach

The developmental approach depends on theories developed by Piaget (1962, 1971) and Kohlberg (1984). They both contributed to the concept of children acquiring particular behaviours and skills at various stages in their development. Piaget (1971) noticed that children interact with human and non-human objects, and it is the relationships they have with these objects that allow them to become progressively more adaptive in their behaviour. As they become more adaptive, they develop higher levels of cognition and start to understand their environment in an increasingly more complex way. Recognition of this development of cognition and acquisition of moral values is important for leaders of children's groups.

Lawrence Kohlberg (1984) was interested in the relationship between Piaget's concepts of cognitive development and the acquisition of moral values. Leaders of children's groups need to have an understanding of the normal developmental sequence in which children come to understand moral concepts (see chapter 3), because a child's decision-making processes will be based on the child's moral understanding and expectations of particular outcomes.

When using a developmental approach, leaders of children's groups need to have expectations about change and outcomes consistent with the group members' levels of development. To bring about change, leaders need to provide opportunities that progressively extend the child's cognitive, social, emotional and moral development.

TYPES OF GROUP

Regardless of the type of group, it is essential that leaders are qualified to use the theoretical approach of their choice and are receiving ongoing professional supervision. It is also desirable that they have specialist training specific to the particular needs of group members. The six types of group previously listed will now be discussed.

Therapy groups

Generally, therapy groups target children who have been diagnosed with a mental health disorder. They are most useful for children suffering from severe emotional distress and/or psychiatric disturbance; for example, children suffering from post-traumatic stress disorder (Shelby, 1994), children with schizophrenia (Speers and Lansing, 1965), children with anxiety disorders, depressive disorders, disruptive behaviour disorders, conduct disorder, oppositional defiant disorder and specific developmental disorder (Gupta, Hariton and Kernberg, 1996).

Generally, the purpose of therapy groups is to attempt to alleviate specific symptoms or problems (for example, depression or anxiety). Their focus is either on identifying and treating emotional and/or psychological difficulties seriously interfering with the child's functioning, and/or addressing developmental and social problems. Therapy groups are remedial, help to promote personal adjustment and are reconstructive.

The theoretical approach adopted in therapy groups will depend primarily on the training and theoretical orientation of the group leader. The leader may use a psychoanalytic, experiential, postmodern, cognitive-behavioural, behavioural or developmental approach. When working with homogeneous groups, many leaders are more likely to adhere strongly to one particular approach. For example, when working with children with specific developmental disorders, a developmental approach is most likely to be used. However, many practitioners will integrate ideas from more than one approach when working with children in groups, particularly when the groups are heterogeneous. For example, a therapist who primarily works from an experiential focus may well use some behaviourist strategies to manage inappropriate behaviour in a heterogeneous group of children.

We recognise that many practitioners have strong prejudices for and/or against particular approaches. We need to respect the many differing viewpoints, recognising that change in children may be achieved in different ways. More research is needed to identify the relative effectiveness of various therapeutic approaches when working with children in groups who have common mental health disorders.

The leadership style and structure of a group will depend on the theoretical approach used. For example, when using a psychoanalytic approach, the group leader will tend to be non-directive and will observe and interpret observed interactions and behaviours. When using an experiential therapies approach the group leader will be much more interactive and will orchestrate the work of the group. Such a leader will use creative experiments to help members experience and understand the meaning of their behaviours.

17

Counselling groups

Life for children is a developmental process during which they are confronted by new situations and/or experiences. Felner *et al.* (1983) point out that children and adolescents inevitably experience many stressors as a consequence of life transitions. The also have to deal with the stressors associated with their need for personal identity and self-esteem (Lopez, 1991). How they think about and cope with these stressors is an important focus of counselling groups (Cowen *et al.*, 1989; Bilides, 1990, 1992).

Group counselling is usually helpful for children who are experiencing some difficulty in coping with the stressors produced by life's challenges. Leaders try to help participants reduce the impact of excessive amounts of stress that have the potential to produce significant undesirable health and mental health consequences (Vogel and Vernberg, 1993).

Counselling groups primarily focus on the exploration and resolution of troubling issues, so that the children involved can modify their beliefs, attitudes and behaviours. They are also useful for preventing the development of problems. Participants have the opportunity to share personal experiences, thoughts and feelings. They may also receive support, encouragement and feedback relating to their issues, behaviours, beliefs and attitudes, as a result of which members may discover more about themselves and realise they have more choice than they thought with regard to changing their behaviours and attitudes.

Ideas from the psychoanalytic, experiential, post-modern and cognitive behavioural approaches may all be relevant to counselling groups for children. Some leaders prefer to use only one of these approaches, whereas others will use an integrative approach incorporating ideas from more than one theoretical model.

Many leaders of counselling groups prefer to use an experiential approach because this approach has synergy with the child's experience of being in a group and consequently maximises the opportunities for experiential learning. Experiential learning is useful in helping group members develop appropriate social relationship skills. A 'here and now' focus can encourage experimentation and the practice of new behaviours. Leaders who use an experiential approach are likely to behave as active members of the group and seek a balance between being at times non-directive and at other times directive. They may self-disclose and share personal information about themselves if they believe this will enhance the group's experience. There may be a strong emphasis on the use of group experience to generate behavioural change.

Some leaders choose to use a cognitive–behavioural interactive approach when running a counselling group, making extensive use of systematic problem solving (Rose, S.D., 1998). Counselling groups are often heterogeneous even though they may target a specific population. For example, a group which targets children who witnessed domestic violence may include some children who present with externalising behaviours and others who present with internalising behaviours, in response to their experiences.

Counselling groups, like other groups, need to be purposeful. Consequently, children who join counselling groups need to be told in advance what the focus of the group will be and why they will be attending.

Psycho-educational groups

Psycho-educational groups may be either or both of the following:

1. Aimed at changing behavioural and emotional responses by exploring values and beliefs and teaching new ways of thinking and behaving.
2. Primarily prevention oriented, helping children to avoid the development of problems, or to learn strategies for coping with future situations which might present difficulties.

It is natural for children to actively develop ideas and concepts to help them make sense of their world. In other words they form *constructs* to describe their environment. As their experiences widen, their original constructs may no longer make sense, so they will replace some of these constructs with new ones. During this process it is useful for them to have information from both adults and peers. Psycho-educational groups provide an opportunity for helping children learn and develop healthy constructs, and consequently to change their attitudes and behaviours so that they may avoid the continuation and/or development of unnecessary problems.

Because psycho-educational groups focus on the acquisition of information and knowledge, these groups are generally more structured than other types of group. They may deliver content in accordance with a structured curriculum. They usually have specifically defined goals and explicit expectations of group members. Although the focus is on learning, the process usually involves group interaction with members of the group sharing and discussing thoughts, feelings, experiences, attitudes, beliefs and values, particularly as these relate to relevant topics. Thus, in a psycho-educational group, group members gain particular knowledge and learn specific skills while participating in a process which includes group interaction and support. Psycho-educational groups rely on strategies and techniques from an educational and a cognitive–behavioural approach. The leader is challenging, directive and didactic.

While counselling groups attempt to modify attitudes and behaviours by helping participants to experience personal growth through sharing, exploring and working through personal issues, psycho-educational groups attempt to change attitudes and behaviours by providing new information and teaching new ways of thinking and behaving. By doing this, the children involved are likely to feel more confident and are able to make better sense of their world and the way in which they respond to it. Thus, an important difference between psycho-educational groups and counselling groups is that in psycho-educational groups the process primarily involves acquiring information to enable learning new ways of thinking and behaving, whereas in counselling groups the method for promoting change focuses primarily on the exploration and resolution of personal issues. What is common between the two types of group is that they both influence the child's thinking, so that changes to cognitive processing occurs and these changes are likely to result in altered behaviours.

Psycho-educational groups can be either homogeneous or heterogeneous.

Personal growth groups

Personal growth groups are intended to help children whose development is not compromised by stress, anxiety or mental health disorder. Their goal is to enhance the child's functioning at both intrapersonal and interpersonal levels. In these groups there is usually a strong emphasis on integrating positive social, spiritual and moral, values, beliefs and attitudes. The intended outcome is to enable children to identify, value and enhance their personal abilities, strengths and skills.

Leaders of personal growth groups generally use strategies from the experiential therapies, and the developmental approach. Their style will often demonstrate a balance between a directive and non-directive approach.

Support groups

The name, 'support group' implies that such a group has been established with the primary goal of providing support. Although the implied central goal of a support group is to provide support, these groups usually produce change in the emotional, cognitive and behavioural state of the children involved.

Support groups are generally established for groups of children who are experiencing similar life challenges. For example, a group might be established to support children whose siblings have a terminal illness or disability.

Leaders of support groups encourage members to become inter-dependent, so that the leader's role becomes less significant as the group progresses, with group members becoming mutually supportive of each other, both during group sessions and out of group sessions. Although initially the group leader will be directive, as the group's life develops, the leader's role becomes more that of a resource person than a typical leader. Leaders may help members to explore their feelings, thoughts and actions and to achieve new levels of understanding about their dilemmas, which lead to more effective and responsible methods of self-management. The main goal of child support groups is to help minimise stress through mutual support and sharing of coping strategies, information and confidence (O'Rourke and Worzbyt, 1996).

In many ways support groups are similar to counselling groups. The main difference is that in support groups the children are selected because of the particular challenges they are facing, whereas in counselling groups the children selected are generally exhibiting emotional or behavioural symptoms of concern. In support groups there is an emphasis on mutual support whereas in counselling groups the emphasis is usually more focused on strengthening the individual child's capacity to personally cope with life's stresses. Consequently, change is promoted.

Examples of groups of children who might benefit by belonging to a support group are the children of alcoholics, latch-key children, children in foster care and children with parents who have a mental health problem.

Support groups are more likely to be heterogeneous than homogeneous.

Developmental skills groups

Developmental skills groups are designed for children whose development is delayed and/or dysfunctional. They may target children where the delay is specific in a particular area such as speech and language or play, or they may target children who have more generalised developmental disabilities. Often children with developmental skills problems will have impaired self-esteem and behavioural problems.

The primary objective of developmental skills groups is to achieve social competence and task mastery in an interactive way. Leaders of these groups need to use a high level of structure to ensure they provide experiences that will result in a positive sense of self, rather than failure experiences that may lead to stress and result in the child seeking relief through avoidance. Along with structure there needs to be flexibility in providing experiences which are marginally ahead of current functioning. This produces stress in the child's interaction with the environment that can be resolved through an extension of personal skills (Downey, 1996).

There needs to be flexibility in the leader's approach to meet the attentional abilities of such children. For example, it may be useful to combine didactic instruction with play and/or activity, and rewards. Generally, sessions should be fairly short because longer periods of time may lead to behavioural regression (Swanson, 1996).

Children in developmental groups are generally less able to be self-reflective and are more oriented to action-based experiential learning. They are more likely to be restricted to the present in their view of themselves and their situation. Consequently, the only therapeutic approaches likely to be successful are the behavioural and developmental approaches.

OPEN AND CLOSED GROUPS

Each of the types of groups described can, if desired, be run as either an open or closed group.

In closed, time-limited, groups the members all join simultaneously and the group runs for a pre-determined number of sessions. Thus all members have the same amount of contact with the group and experience the same programme. Advantages of this are that the group process is apt to be most comfortable for all members as they are likely to have similar experiences of the stages of group development (see chapter 7). Additionally, closed groups provide a climate in which high levels of group cohesion may develop.

Open groups allow new members to join and existing members to leave at different times during the running of the group. This has the advantage that individual children can leave when their goals have been achieved. However, leaders do need to be aware that when children leave an open group, regression in the behaviours of the remaining group may occur, as the departure of some members will be perceived as a loss.

With an open group, when workers identify new potential members they can be included without a long wait for a new programme to start. Additionally, errors in the initial composition of a group can sometimes be corrected by adding new members to achieve a desirable group composition (Rose and Edleson, 1987).

Children who have already experienced belonging to an open group for a while may be able to help newcomers to feel welcome and can help them to understand the group norms. However, leaders need to recognise that there may be issues for existing members when new members are added, particularly if this occurs soon after other members have left and are being missed.

Sometimes new members who join an open group may feel uncomfortable as they move into a group of people who already know each other. Rather than introducing only one new member at a time, it is recommended that two or three children be added at the same time to relieve the pressure on the incoming members (Rose and Edleson, 1987).

Open groups are particularly useful in settings such as refuges, half-way houses, and hospital inpatient settings, where individuals settle in and leave at differing times from each other. Using an open group format can also be useful when running therapy groups. In this case new members may learn from observation and interaction with longer term members who may effectively act as role models, with peer tutoring occurring.

TOPIC-FOCUSED AND SYSTEM-FOCUSED GROUPS

Topic-focused groups target a population of children who have common characteristics and/or experiences, and thus have similar needs. For example, children with social skills problems have common characteristics, and children whose parents have separated and divorced have common experiences. In topic-focused groups the children need to be of compatible developmental levels (see Chapter 3).

System-focused groups are groups of children who belong to a single system. For example, inpatients of a hospital unit for children with mental health disorders, children living in a group home, or sibling groups. In system-focused groups the children in a group may have different developmental levels and different experiences. They may also have differing characteristics.

DECIDING ON THE TYPE OF GROUP AND THEORETICAL APPROACH

While there are differences between the six types of group described, there are also similarities and there is overlap between them. In all six types the primary goal is to facilitate change and learning in individual children. Success in group work sometimes depends on combining essential elements of more than one type of group and on integrating concepts from more than one theoretical approach. For example, when working with children who have witnessed domestic violence, leaders may combine elements of therapy, counselling and psycho-educational groups, so that deep emotional issues are addressed and education regarding both abusive and appropriate behaviours is included. Further, when working with these children the psychoanalytic issues of transference and counter-transference will need to be addressed, and it may be useful to use 'here and now' experiments from the experiential therapies and introduce solution-focused problem-solving from a post-modern approach. For those children who are externalising their responses to their experience of family violence, behavioural strategies may be useful.

It needs to be recognised that some workers are uncomfortable with the idea of using an integrated approach that draws on more than one theoretical model. It is sensible for these workers to stay focused on using a single theoretical approach of their choice.

Leaders need to be fully conversant with the theoretical underpinning of their work, particularly when they are integrating elements from different theoretical approaches. It is essential that they are clear about both their theoretical orientation and the type of group they are running.

PART II

PLANNING A GROUP PROGRAMME

3 Identifying the needs of a target group

Groups can be run for a wide range of reasons such as:

- To address social skills, improve problem solving skills, improve self-esteem and to teach children to play
- For relaxation training, promoting insight, anger management, treating depression
- For children with mental health diagnoses (either as inpatients or outpatients), children with a particular problem (such as ADHD), with specific behaviour problems and substance abuse problems
- For children of alcoholic parents and of separated or divorced parents
- For children who have been, or are part of, violent families, suffer from chronic or terminal illness, have a relative who suffers from chronic or terminal illness, have been, or are at risk of being, sexually abused, suffer from excessive anxiety, have study or other school performance problems

When running groups it is important to target children with similar needs.

To identify the needs of a particular group of children, leaders need to fully research the relevant literature relating to the target group, so they are familiar with current theory and relevant research findings. They can also use information from their own experiences in relation to the target group as well as information provided by other workers with experience in working with a similar group. Leaders also need to have a sound understanding of child development theory so they can make realistic and relevant assumptions about the needs of the target group of children concerned.

FORMULATING ASSUMPTIONS ABOUT THE TARGET GROUP

Once leaders have identified a target group, and have familiarised themselves with information about that group, they can make assumptions about the issues and likely emotional, social and behavioural responses of the children in that group. The process of making relevant assumptions about a target group can be enhanced by using a pre-intervention survey (Dolgin *et al.*, 1997). This survey is carried out before planning the programme to help in determining the needs of the group.

An example of the formulation of assumptions

Consider children who come from families where violence has occurred. Leaders planning to run a group for these children might assume that they are likely to have some, or all, of the following problems (Jaffe *et al.*, 1990; Varma, 1997):

- Issues around family secrets, power and control, shame and embarrassment
- Issues regarding bullying and victimisation and issues of loss (as a consequence of death, separation or emotional unavailabilty)
- Poor self-esteem, poor social skills, poor impulse control and poor problem-solving skills (so they may use violence as a problem-solving technique in school and with peers and family)
- Difficulties in labelling feelings, in expressing feelings appropriately (particularly anger), in identifying the triggers of their anxiety and in recognising their behaviours as a response to anxiety after overwhelming experiences (for example, when they resort to fight or flight)
- They may internalise their anger or have a low and limited tolerance for frustration and act out their anger
- They may have anxiety about their own safety, have intrusive thoughts, experience survivor guilt and lack of validation of their experiences
- They may have distorted values regarding violence in society, confusion about whether abuse is okay or not, continuation of abuse patterns in their own lives, difficulty in understanding who is responsible for violence and confusion about gender roles and attributes
- They may experience depression, stress disorders, psychosomatic complaints, be emotionally dependent (that is, be at high risk of using alcohol or drugs, of running away and of sexual acting out) and have insecure attachment to a primary carer

- They may frequently absent themselves from school and may experience social isolation
- They may have difficulty in using healing processes such as play, dream-work or community support

It must be remembered that these assumptions, although generally true for children from violent families, may, or may not, be entirely correct for the children in a particular group. It is helpful, however, to use these assumptions initially when devising a programme, and to revise them using an action research model. The action research model allows for modification to the group programme as new information emerges about the children in a particular group (Carr and Kemmis, 1986).

The listed assumptions about children from violent families would be useful in helping leaders identify the needs of these children. Similarly, in order to determine the likely needs of the children in any target group, leaders can start by making assumptions about the children concerned. These assumptions can then be used to identify likely needs in conjunction with information about normal child development.

Leaders need to have an understanding of normal child development. This understanding is not only useful in helping leaders determine the needs of a particular target group, but is also useful because the developmental levels of the children involved will undoubtedly affect the type of group to be run, the degree of structure needed and the leader's expectations of likely group processes.

NORMAL CHILD DEVELOPMENT

In this section, a brief over-view of normal child development is provided. Readers who would like to understand child development more fully can refer to Berndt (1997) or Santrock (1996). Important aspects of children's development relevant to their inclusion in particular groups include moral development, emotional development, social development, sexual development, cognitive development and motor development.

Moral development

The field of moral development has been characterised by a broad range of views. The diversity of views is a consequence of contributions coming from several different perspectives, including cognitive developmental, behavioural/learning, personality, social and cultural perspectives (Kurtines and Gewirtz, 1995). Although there have been many different points of view, much of the discussion has centred around the work of Lawrence Kohlberg (1984) which draws strongly from the cognitive developmental perspective. Although others have disagreed in some respects with Kohlberg's understanding of moral development, his work has played a pivotal role in understanding moral development (Kurtines and Gewirtz, 1995). We will therefore give an outline of Kohlberg's (1984) stages of moral judgment followed by additional information from other perspectives which suggest that his stages need modification when targeting specific behavioural, cultural or social groups.

Kohlberg's stages of moral development

Kohlberg (1984) proposed that moral awareness develops in a sequence of six stages. While movement through the stages is always towards a higher level of morality, progression is not automatic.

Stage one – 'Avoid punishment' orientation: At this stage children respond to rules and are concerned about how authority figures will react to them, whether they will be punished or rewarded, and whether they will be labelled good or bad. This stage is usually present at the age of two-and-a-half to seven years.

Stage two – 'Self benefit' orientation: In this stage children realise that each individual has an idea of what is right or best. They are concerned with the needs and motives of others and with the idea that one good (or bad) turn deserves another. Many children between the ages of seven and twelve demonstrate this stage of development.

Stage three – 'Acceptance by others' orientation: In this stage young people can recognise other people's points of view. They are influenced by the feelings of others, by what others expect and approve of, and by beliefs about what a virtuous person should do. This stage of development is typical for a young person in the pre-adolescent stage of development.

Stage four – 'Maintain the social order' orientation: At this stage young people consider 'right' as what is best for society. They value doing their duty and respect for authority and rules are perceived as morally appropriate behaviour. This stage of development often begins to emerge towards the end of adolescence.

Stage five – 'Contract fulfilment' orientation: In this stage people respect impartial laws and agree to abide by them. They believe that laws should be changed when they infringe on human rights. If they disobey an unjust law they may willingly suffer the consequences. This stage is often in evidence during late adolescent and the early adult stage of development.

Stage six – 'Ethical principle' orientation: Conscience is the directing agent at this stage, based on universal ethical principles. Action must be good in itself and consistent with these principles. While many adults attempt to achieve this stage of moral development, few ever reach it.

Social and cultural perspectives on moral development

Gilligan (1986) alleged that Kohlberg's (1984) theory down-scored females' moral reasoning because it tended to undervalue the care orientation which she saw as synonymous with female moral reasoning. However, a two-year longitudinal study by Walker (1989) failed to support the notion that Kohlberg's (1984) theory is biased against the care orientation. Consequently, group leaders should not expect that female children will have a higher level of concern for looking after the needs of others in a group than male children.

Snarey (1995) suggests that Kohlberg's (1984) theory does not take sufficient account of social class and cultural variations in moral reasoning. He believed that moral development needed to take account of values such as the community voice evident in some working-class and non-urban communities and cultural groups (Snarey, 1993). An example of the values referred to by Snarey (1993) is the concept of doing favours, which he considered to be a primary means of building and maintaining relationships within working-class communities. He believed that working-class people typically view such informal exchanges as expressions of good citizenship, faithfulness and loyalty. In contrast, members of the middle class typically view such exchanges suspiciously, characterising them as crude and covert. As a consequence, misinterpretations might occur in stage four of Kohlberg's (1984) model.

Additionally, Snarey and Kelijo (1991) identified six concepts which are not addressed, or are misunderstood, in Kohlberg's (1984) model when considering people from working-class and village backgrounds. These include the following:

- Happiness of the individual, which is integrally linked to the well-being of the community
- Tradition, which seems to fulfil the role of law and is either parallel or superior to the legal system
- Understanding, where mutual understanding is integral to the community
- Reciprocity, i.e. doing favours as a means of building and maintaining relationships
- Role relationships and solidarity, where norms and customs associated with the role are recognised
- Unity of life, where concepts are related to the understanding that community needs take precedence over individual needs

Behavioural/learning perspectives on moral development

One behavioural/learning perspective implies that moral behaviour is primarily learnt by watching others through observation, modelling, and imitation (Bandura, 1971). Some factors involved include:

- Similarity of the model to the observer
- Status of the model
- Degree of nurturance of the model
- Vicarious learning by observing the outcomes of others behaviour
- The role of reward and punishment as motivating performance

The behavioural/learning perspective is extremely useful when considering groups for children who have come from families where violence has been, or is, occurring.

Personality perspectives on moral development

The personality perspective focuses on understanding the total person with the concept of personal identity being central (Kurtines and Gewirtz, 1995). This perspective views morality as a by-product of personality and believes that the primary issue is to identify and understand the developmental origins of attitudes to authority, responsiveness to the needs and expectations of others and the nature of the arguments individuals use to justify their moral orientation (Hogan and Emler, 1995).

Emotional development

Three stages of emotional development will be considered; from two-and-a-half to five years, from six to nine years and from nine to twelve years. In considering these three stages it should be recognised that emotional development is influenced by various factors including temperament, social and environmental influences and the child's resilience.

Current work in behavioural genetics suggests that many if not most characteristics of human beings (including intelligence, personality, attitudes and beliefs and psychopathology) are strongly influenced by inheritance (Plomin, 1989). These inherited characteristics contribute to the child's temperament. Most researchers agree that temperament results in individual behavioural differences in emotional expressiveness (Braungart et al., 1992). Consequently, group leaders need to be aware that children of similar developmental age may express their emotions quite differently. It also needs to be recognised that, as found by Freedman (1969), there are temperamental differences in children cross-culturally.

There is clear evidence of the importance of environmental factors in determining development. For example, a child's emotional development will be affected by the socio-economic status and/or the type of family in which the child is reared. Owens (1993) suggests that possible differences between children who grow up in dual wage earner families, single parent families, or blended families may need to be taken into account. In the preschool years, child-rearing styles and parent–child interaction have been noted as being particularly important for development in general (Clarke-Stewart, 1988) and behaviour problems in particular (Campbell, 1990).

The child's resilience will also influence emotional development. Resilience involves the child's ability to withstand or recover quickly from difficult conditions. How children learn to cope with the stresses inherent in the normal course of development will in part determine that child's developmental trajectory (Schroeder and Gordon, 1991). Pinpointing stress events in children's lives is difficult. What may be thought of as a negative event or situation by some children may not be perceived that way by all children. Currently there is a shift in focus from major events as stressors (divorce, death of a parent, moving) to the ongoing stresses and strains of daily life (home work, exams, arguments with family and friends) (Dubow *et al.*, 1991).

Emotional development characteristics of the preschool child (two and a half to five years)

At this stage many children experience fairly fluid emotions with rapid changes from feeling independent to becoming clingy, from feeling secure to feeling insecure, and from feeling affectionate to becoming hostile. They like to win at games, and they experience jealousy and sibling rivalry. Commonly, many young pre-school children develop fears (for example, fears of physical vulnerability, of death and of loneliness). They may have difficulty in distinguishing fantasy from reality. At the end of the pre-school period children can usually begin to translate thoughts and feelings into words and actions.

Emotional development characteristics of the six to nine year old child

At this stage most children are gaining a sense of competence and are eager to please, but seek reassurance through praise and recognition. Generally, children at this stage are beginning to separate from parents and to seek an independent identity. Six to nine year old children tend to be less egocentric, can see themselves with some objectivity and can imagine themselves in someone else's place. They are usually somewhat afraid of frightening or distressing stories and television series.

Typically, from the age of seven years onwards many fears are still present (for example, fears of thunder, man-made noises, ghosts, or of someone under the bed).

Children over eight are more likely to sense aggression from others. Magic and make-believe become increasingly private affairs. Children of this age measure themselves against societal standards set by adults and peer groups. In this period children tend to be sensitive to ridicule, criticism, failure and fears of unpleasant social situations (such as being sent to the principal's office). Most children of this age are alert to the feelings of others but may use insight to injure others. Feelings of sibling jealousy continue, but mostly around issues of justice (for example, bedtime rules). Children over the age of eight tend to cry less, but may burst into tears especially when tired, hurt or criticised.

Emotional development characteristics of the pre-adolescent (nine to twelve years)

With this group there is a strong continuation of developmental characteristics begun in middle childhood. There is growing concern and curiosity about sex and developing crushes and hero-worshipping. Many children display perfectionist tendencies, setting unrealistically high standards for themselves with subsequent or consequent feelings of frustration when these are not achieved. There is a strong move towards independence and separateness, but a passionate dependence on best friends. The child of this age is still close to parents, which may lead to some ambivalence. The search or move towards independence involves exploring unknown places, rebellion and answering back. Generally fears and worries about fantasies reduce, although there may be increased anxiety with regard to school achievements and social and personal issues.

The child at this age may experience regression in conflict or stress situations. Typically girls may cry and have emotional outbursts and boys may become sullen and sulky.

Social development

Three stages of social development will be considered at ages two-and-a-half to five years, six to nine years and nine to twelve years. However, it needs to be recognised that these stages will be significantly influenced by a number of environmental factors. Important environmental factors include attendance at daycare, peer interaction, culture, television and the school setting.

The influence of attendance at day care on social development

Daycare can have both positive and negative effects on social development (Belsky, 1988; Belsky and Steinberg 1982). Andersson (1989)

37

found that those children who entered daycare as infants were more socially competent, cooperative, persistent and independent then late-entry and home-reared children. Belsky (1988) found that children who had experienced daycare were more peer-oriented than home-reared children. Vlietstra (1982) found that full-day preschool children, compared with half-day children, interacted more with their peers and displayed more pro-social as well as aggressive and assertive behaviours. Increased interaction may have provided greater opportunities for conflict, leading to more aggressive behaviours. Some studies have shown that children with extensive daycare experience tend to be less cooperative with adults, more active and somewhat more aggressive toward their peers and teachers (Siegal and Storey, 1985).

There appears to be a growing consensus that the quality of daycare programmes is a salient factor in influencing children's adjustment (Andersson, 1992).

The influence of peer groups on social development

Clearly a child's family has a major influence on his or her social development. Perhaps the next most important influence is the child's peer group. Children learn from their peer interaction how to control and regulate their behaviour. Additionally, peers may strengthen existing behaviours and attitudes, help the child establish new ones or weaken those that are in conflict with peer-group values (Owens, 1993).

The influence of culture on social development

The priorities set by the cultural environment in which children grow up influence parents and teachers in selecting certain behaviours while neglecting others, so that children acquire behaviours valued and relevant for the particular culture. For example, in some Asian communities behaviours that are valued tend to centre around a collectivist philosophy where cooperation and interrelatedness with others and group orientation are important. In contrast, western culture tends to emphasise an individualistic philosophy where socialisation focuses on raising autonomous, self-reliant, independent individuals (Owens, 1993).

The influence of television

Another important influence in social development is television. Unfortunately, some children watch an inordinate amount of television and this behaviour is often established in early childhood. Watching television can increase both pro-social and aggressive behaviour, perpetuate stereotypic notions about social groups and be persuasive in influencing children's food, toy and clothing preferences.

The influence of school

School is not just an educational institution but also a social institution, reflecting the culture of which it is a part and transmitting to the young an ethos and a world-view as well as imparting specific skills and knowledge. Because children spend years in school as members of a small society in which there are tasks to be done, others to relate to, and rules that define acceptable and unacceptable behaviours, the school environment has a strong influence on many aspects of social attitudes and behaviours influencing the sense of self, beliefs about competency and morality and the child's concepts of a social system beyond the family (Owens, 1993).

Social development characteristics of the preschool child (two-and-a-half to five years)

At this age many children tend to be easy-going, compliant and cooperative, especially in play. There is a growing sense of identity within and outside the family and a sense of sex role. Often children's speech tends to be self-centred while they are beginning to see other children as individual and to communicate directly with them. There is generally a heightened interest in using words that shock, and frequent arguments and tantrums particularly in the early part of this stage.

In groups, frequent shifts in group leadership are common, and play groups are loosely formed and easily disbanded. There may be a strong emphasis on socio-dramatic play with others (that is, imaginative pretend play). The child is likely to begin to learn to distinguish fantasy from reality, and there is a developing sense of self-reliance and independence. Friends become valued for, their material possessions (for example, 'He's my friend because he has a swing set'.

Social development characteristics of six to nine year olds

Social development at this stage is characterised by a move away from the family and towards external socialisation. The peer group is a key source of identity where clothes, toys, interests and outings become important. Group membership gives security and the child becomes part of a sub-culture with its own rules, values, codes and rituals.

Individuals tend to be selective about close friends. They may seek semi-permanent friends and make enemies. Children begin to understand that feelings and intentions keep friends together, not just material possessions. They also take into account their own needs. Best friends are usually of the same sex.

Children of this age like organised sport in small groups and there is an over-concern with rules and teams. Most children of this age like competition and enjoy engaging in activities such as sport, team games and spelling bees. It is normal for children of this age not to like to lose at games and to cheat when playing games. There is usually a sex-related division of interests.

From the age of seven onwards many children become self-critical. They see themselves with a social role (for example, school pupil), and there is a focus on learning manners and social skills in formal situations. There is an increasing interest in possessions (as a consequence they like to have money and payment for chores). Generally, the social behaviour of children of this age reflects a time of more give and take and more possible negotiation in conflict situations.

Social development of the pre-adolescent

Most children at this stage are aware of a third person perspective. They can distance themselves from both parties in a relationship and study it as a whole. Experiencing problems and conflicts with a friend does not necessarily result in the end of the friendship.

In this stage many young people move toward becoming more outgoing and making more friends. There is also an increased interest in the opposite sex. Peer groups replace adults with regard to the setting of behaviour standards. The young person's self-esteem depends on how they think their friends perceive them.

Sexual development

It is common knowledge that preschool children are very curious about their own and others' bodies and that, given the opportunity, they will engage in sexual exploration of other children (Gundersen *et al.*, 1981). It has also been demonstrated that sexual exploration of adults is very common among children between the age of two to four and that although this touching behaviour decreases with increasing age, some eight to ten year old children intermittently attempt to continue this behaviour (Rosenfeld *et al.*, 1986). The issue of when the awareness of sexuality as an interactive behaviour begins, however, is clouded by cultural attitudes and values about children and sexuality. Despite the fact that children are known to engage in sexual behaviour alone and in interaction with others from an early age, their awareness of sexuality is in part a function of their knowledge of sexual facts and their understanding of sexual behaviour.

In societies where sexuality is treated openly, children tend to have more sexual experience at an earlier age, and are also likely to be exposed to sex education earlier and to a greater extent than in societies with more restrictive attitudes. Thus, these children would be expected to have more knowledge of sexuality (Schroeder and Gordon, 1991). However the relationship between children's knowledge of sexuality and their sexual behaviour is not clear. It appears that in the area of sexuality, more experience is not necessarily accompanied by greater understanding (Gordon *et al.*, 1990).

Girls have been found to know more about sexuality than boys at an early age. Young children's concerns about sexual intercourse or other adult sexual behaviours appears to be rare in children not involved in, or exposed to, such behaviours (Waterman, 1986).

When considering the sexual development of children it should be noted that studies of children's knowledge of sexuality have found a developmental progression related to cognitive development and that children's knowledge of sexuality increases with age (Bem, 1989).

Clearly, there will be considerable differences in children's sexual development. There are, however, a number of stages of sexual development which are commonly experienced by many children. These will now be described.

Common behaviours of the two-and-a-half year old

The child shows interest in different postures of boys and girls urinating and is interested in the physical differences between the sexes.

Common behaviours of the three year old

The child verbally expresses interest in physical differences between sexes and in different postures in urinating. Girls may attempt to urinate standing up and boys sitting down.

Common behaviours of the four year old

The child may become extremely conscious of the navel. As a consequence of social stress they may grab their genitals and may need to urinate. They play the game of 'show' and may be verbally expressive about elimination. They demand privacy for themselves but may be very interested in the bathroom activity of others. They are interested in other people's bathrooms.

Common behaviours of the five year old

The child is familiar with, but not very interested in, the physical differences between the sexes. There may be less sex play and games of 'show', less exposing of self, less bathroom play and a lower interest in unfamiliar bathrooms.

Common behaviours of the six year old

The child may exhibit a marked interest in the differences between sexes in body structure and may ask questions regarding these differences. Practical answers to questions about sex differences may be discovered through mutual investigation.

There may be mild sex play and/or exhibitionism in play, or in school toilets, including games of 'show'. Children may play 'hospitals' and pretend to take rectal temperature. Giggling, calling names and remarks involving words dealing with elimination may occur.

Where children are subjected to sex play by older children, the age and power differences between the children are critical in defining this as normal sex play or as exploitation and abuse.

Common behaviours of the seven year old

The child may have less interest in sex. There may be some mutual exploration, experimentation and sex play, but less than earlier.

Common behaviours of the eight year old

Interest in sex may be fairly high, though sexual exploration in play is less common than at six. There may be an interest in peeping, smutty jokes and provocative giggling. Children whisper, write and spell elimination and/or sex words.

Common behaviours of nine and ten year olds

The child may talk about sex information with friends of the same sex and show an interest in details of their own organs and functions. The child may seek out pictures in books. Use of sexual words and swearing may occur and sex poems begin. There will be considerable interest in smutty jokes.

Cognitive and motor development

Cognitive and motor development in relation to tasks which need to be achieved will be discussed for the stages of infancy and childhood, mid-childhood and adolescence.

Tasks of infancy and early childhood

General achievement of physiological stability and the understanding of sex differences occurs in this stage. The formation of simple concepts of social and physical reality occurs. Expectations of high levels of reasoning ability are unrealistic.

Learning to walk, take solid food, talk and control the elimination of body wastes are the primary tasks of children of this age.

Tasks of middle childhood (6 years to 12 years)

In middle childhood children are learning physical skills necessary for ordinary games. They learn to get along with mates of their own age and are intent on building wholesome attitudes towards themselves as growing organisms. This is an extremely productive time in terms of developing the fundamental skills of reading, writing and calculating, and for the general development of concepts necessary for everyday living. The child's reasoning ability does not include complex abstract thinking, but does include the ability to use metaphor and symbols.

Tasks of adolescents

Achieving new and more mature relationships with mates of the same age and of both sexes is of major importance at this stage. Adolescents' thoughts and energy tend to be focused on ensuring masculine or feminine social roles, accepting their physique and using their bodies effectively. They begin to develop new cognitive skills which include abstract reasoning and understanding physical and social inter-relationships. These new skills help improve strategies for coping with stressors and everyday issues. Adolescents are beginning, and continue, to acquire sets of values and ethical systems to guide their behaviour. They develop an ideology which prepares them for marriage, family life and an economic career.

THE INFLUENCE OF DEVELOPMENTAL LEVEL OF FUNCTIONING

The significance of children's developmental level of functioning depends on whether the group concerned is a topic-focused or system-focused group (see Chapter 2).

In system-focused groups, children of differing developmental age may be included, provided that leaders understand and make allowance for developmental differences. The leader's expectations of individual children will depend on developmental functioning.

Topic-focused groups generally consist of members who are within a compatible developmental range. When determining the likely needs of group members, leaders need to use information from the assumptions made about the target group in conjunction with knowledge of the relevant developmental level.

Why developmental level is important in assessing needs

There are two important reasons why it is essential to consider the children's developmental levels of functioning when considering whether group work is suitable for the children concerned. These are:

1. To function effectively a group of children in a topic-focused group need to have the same capabilities and skills.
2. To meet the children's needs, a group programme must be able to address the children's issues at their developmental level.

Individual children respond to issues and crises in different ways at different ages. The way children understand their world at age five is quite different from the way they understand their world at age ten. Consequently, children who have been exposed to the same experiences may have quite different needs if they are of different developmental ages.

An illustrative example

Let us reconsider children who come from families where there has been violence. A child who is aged seven to nine is likely to have needs that are different from a child who is aged nine and above.

Children from violent families between the ages of seven and nine: For these children social contacts away from the family home have an increasing importance. Consequently these children may notice that other families live without the family conflict they have experienced. However, their experiences of victimisation and misuse of power may also have distorted their beliefs regarding male–female relationships, rules and self-image. The trauma, internal conflicts and poor modelling these children have been exposed to are likely to have affected their social relationships, and social relationships are particularly important for their age group. It is therefore not uncommon for such children to demand immediate gratification, have a low tolerance for frustration and a decreased attention span. This often results in explosive conflicts at school and with siblings. Seven to nine year olds bring with them the task of understanding rules. Consequently the rules that exist in the family home may present confusion for the child when compared with those in their wider social framework.

The needs of these children are:

1. To re-construct their beliefs around male–female relationships.
2. To learn alternative ways of responding to others in conflict situations.
3. To understand that the rules and consequences at home, can not be generalised into the wider society.

Children from violent families aged nine to adolescence: Having recognised that their own families are different, these children often feel as though their family is, to some extent, isolated and separate from the outside world. Much of their understanding of social behaviour is based on their observations of maladaptive behaviour. They may feel isolated and have a need to be secretive. They may be jealous of other children who have more comfortable lives. They may begin to act out the gender roles which they learnt at home in their peer relationships. Moral development at this age does allow the child to confront questions regarding responsibility for behaviour, and they are likely to question the motives and intentions of others. They are likely to learn to cope by using maladaptive responses such as blame or guilt which inevitably affects their self-concept and self-esteem, and they may either externalise or internalise their responses.

The needs of these children are:

1. To deal with the stigmatisation of coming from a violent family.
2. To develop different social skills in relating to peers of the opposite sex.
3. To develop a healthy self-concept which is not based on family stereotypes.

This illustrative example demonstrates the way in which children's needs depend not only on their experiences or psychological condition, but also on their developmental age. Thus when planning groups for children it is essential for leaders to take into account the interaction between the child's experiences and/or psychological condition, and the child's developmental age, when determining needs.

4 Planning to run a group

The first step in deciding whether or not to run a group is to identify a target group in which the children have common needs. Leaders can then make assumptions about children in the target group under consideration. From these assumptions they can identify the likely needs of these children as described in Chapter 3. It is then necessary to decide whether a group treatment option could address the identified needs. If so, and if it is thought that running a group would be the best approach, then leaders need to determine whether it is practicable to run such a group. Once it has been determined that it is practicable to run a group, a timetable outlining each stage of the planning process needs to be drawn up and an overall plan prepared.

DECIDING WHETHER A GROUP TREATMENT OPTION COULD MEET IDENTIFIED NEEDS

When considering group treatment options leaders need to take into account both the type of group which is most suitable and the theoretical framework to be used (see Chapter 2). For example, consider a target group of children aged between nine and twelve years whose parents have a mental illness. There are several options which might address the needs of such children. Among these options are a counselling group with a psychoanalytic or experiential framework, where the children's intra- and inter-personal issues could be addressed. An alternative would be a psycho-educational group using a cognitive behavioural framework, in which the children would gain helpful information about mental health disorders and learn new strategies for coping.

The type of group selected, and the theoretical framework used, are certain to be a reflection of the leaders' preferences, skills and training. In this book the emphasis will be on topic-focused groups which tend to be structured.

DECIDING WHETHER IT IS PRACTICABLE TO RUN A GROUP

When deciding whether or not it is practicable to run a group the following need to be taken into consideration:

- Availability of suitable leaders
- Number of children available to join the group
- Location
- Length of individual sessions and overall duration
- Financial cost
- Timing

Availability of suitable leaders

We believe it is usually preferable, and often essential, to have two leaders for each group. This is particularly true when running groups for highly active or aggressive children and when running groups for young children below the age of nine or ten. Having two leaders does involve extra cost but the advantages are substantial. There can certainly be disadvantages in having only one leader.

A major disadvantage of having only one leader is that one person cannot attend to the needs of the whole group and simultaneously attend to the needs of individual children who may be in need of personal help. For example, while a group is in progress a child may act out, become distressed and need individual attention, or may need to be taken to get a drink or go to the toilet. Where there are two leaders, one can continue to attend to the group while the other attends to individual children who have special needs at particular times.

When selecting leaders it is important to consider gender issues. With some groups it can be useful to have one female and one male facilitator. This has the advantage that appropriate female and male role behaviours and ways of relating can be modelled. However, there are particular target groups where it may be more appropriate – or essential for some groups – to have facilitators of one particular gender (for example when working with girls who have been sexually abused by males).

Where two leaders of opposite sex work together they may symbolically represent a parental couple capable of dealing with the most vulnerable feelings in the group. Above all, having two leaders is excellent for dealing with, and containing, the grief and anger in a group, as children who have experienced particularly traumatic environments and recurring episodes of abandonment may be able to hate one leader without feeling that their whole world has been destroyed (McCormack and Sinason, 1996).

In any group, at least one of the leaders should have experience of working in a group with children of the relevant age. It is also desirable, although not essential, that at least one of the leaders should have experience of working with children who fit the criteria for the target group.

Number of children available to join the group

If running a group is to be practicable there need to be sufficient children from the selected target population available to join the group so that the group will be of workable size and cost effective.

Location

The group room needs to have sufficient space and be suitably furnished to allow for the planned activities to be carried out. The room should preferably be free from visual and auditory distractions from outside, and should not contain materials which could be distracting. It should be a contained space so that children are safe and cannot wander off, as well as ensuring that privacy and confidentiality can be maintained. Ideally, the room should provide a warm and welcoming ambience with colourful furnishings and comfortable seating arrangements. For some types of group, bean bags and cushions may be suitable, whereas for other types, particularly where the group programme relies heavily on verbal interaction, more formal seating arrangements may be appropriate.

In institutional and educational settings, it may be advantageous to locate the group in a place that has a degree of separateness from the main areas of activity. Symbolically, this enables the children to recognise that within the group there may be a different set of norms, particularly with regard to freedom of expression. In school settings it is especially important for group leaders to take account of issues concerning stigmatisation and privacy when selecting a location.

Geographically, the location should be easy for parents or carers to access, especially if the group plans to meet more than once a week. Attention needs to be given to the availability of parking and the convenience of public transport. The provision of a safe waiting space for parents, carers and siblings is required, as parents and carers may arrive early when delivering or collecting children.

Length of individual sessions and overall duration

The number of group sessions required and the length of each session will depend on the needs of the target group and the age range (the relevance of these factors when planning a programme will be considered in Chapter 5). Schnitzer de Neuhaus (1985) suggests that generally young school age children can only handle forty-five minutes in a group, while for older children sixty to ninety minutes may be acceptable. While agreeing that this may be true for those groups which rely heavily on verbal interaction with little activity, we have found that for most children, one-and-a-half hours, or even two hours, can be a comfortable length for a group, providing the group programme is designed as described in Chapter 5. Many group leaders believe groups for children should be limited to a maximum of two hours. However, for some target groups there can be advantages in running a group for an extended period, such as over two whole days at a weekend or all day on a number of consecutive Saturdays. Groups run during school holidays have the advantage that intensive work can be carried out if these groups are run on a daily basis. Where long group sessions are used the nature of the group's activities needs to be such that interest is maintained throughout the day. The group programme then becomes rather like an intensive workshop.

Generally, from eight to ten weeks duration seems to be the minimum useful length for groups that meet for one or two hours each week. This length of programme may then fit within school terms and will allow adequate time for introduction and termination sessions. It also allows for satisfactory progress through the stages of group development (Chapter 7).

For some children and for psychoanalytic groups, long term therapy is considered optimal, with groups running from a minimum of several months up to twelve months. For children with a developmental disability, the process of achieving positive outcomes in

51

mastery of tasks and skills is slow, so long term group work is required.

Open groups (see Chapter 2) generally run continuously for extended periods, so that members can leave when goals have been achieved and new members may join at any time without delay.

In topic-focused groups, where the group programme addresses specific issues or needs of the target population of children, it may be useful for some members to repeat a group programme.

Financial cost

There are a number of costs to be considered when deciding whether or not it is feasible to run a group programme. Costs may relate to staff time, hire of a venue, hire of equipment (such as audio-visual equipment), purchasing or hire of books, tapes, and materials required for use in the group, cost of refreshments, cost of childcare for siblings (if required) and other costs including photocopying, stationery, advertising and mailing expenses.

Often staff costs are underestimated by agencies interested in running groups for children. It does need to be recognised that the cost of staff time is one of the major expenses incurred when running a group. This need to be considered so that accurate justification for running a group on economic grounds can be achieved. The total cost of running a group can then be compared with the costs involved if the children were helped individually.

Staff time is needed, not just for the time spent in the group, but also for the activities described later in connection with preparing an overall plan.

Timing

When considering whether or not it is practicable to run a group, account should be taken of timing, as this can be critical to the success of a group. For children living in the community, the chosen day of the week and the time of day will influence the ability of parents or carers to bring their children to a group. Leaders need to consider whether attending a group will adversely interfere with school and other activities. If a group is being designed to complement another programme or treatment option, the timing needs to be compatible with the other programme or treatment option.

Leaders may need to liaise with other agencies to determine the likely usefulness of a proposed programme. Clearly, it will not be sensible to duplicate programmes unless an existing programme is over-subscribed.

Consideration needs to be given as to whether the proposed group programme will run during a public holiday or major holiday period. For some programmes there will be advantages in running a group during a vacation, whereas for others there will be disadvantages.

For system-based groups, that is those where children in the target group are located in a residential facility, institution or hospital, daily groups may be possible. These allow for continuous work of an intensive nature.

PREPARING AN OVERALL PLAN

As indicated previously, before deciding to run a group, leaders need to determine whether it will be both practicable and cost effective. Once this has been determined, then careful planning is needed to ensure there is adequate time to organise the necessary human and material resources and to put into effect the required processes described in this and subsequent chapters. The price for lack of thorough and thoughtful planning is high. Frequently it is paid in groups which terminate prematurely, groups in which attendance of members is sporadic and irregular and groups that are felt by practitioners and group members to have failed in meeting the needs of group members (Fatout, 1996).

Table 4.1 shows a sequence of tasks which needs to be carried out when running groups for children. It is helpful to estimate the hours, days, or weeks required in order to carry out each of the tasks listed. These tasks will now be discussed.

Drawing up a timetable

Readers may wish to complete Table 4.1 as the basis for a planning timetable by entering times required for each task in the left hand

Table 4.1   Planning guide

Hours, days or weeks required	Task
	Draw up a timetable with dates for each stage of the whole process. This needs to include time for planning, for assessment and for selection of group members, for running the programme, and for evaluation of the programme.
	Plan details of the overall programme and individual sessions
	Plan the intake procedure
	Plan and organise the practical arrangements (for example, organising equipment and furniture required).
	Prepare and organise advertising (if required) including form letters and consent forms.
	Organise and carry out an intake procedure.
	Assessment of possible group members and their parents
	Notify successful and unsuccessful applicants
	Supervisor and leader/s to meet to work out roles, etc.
	Preparation before individual sessions
	Run the group sessions
	Clear up and debrief after group sessions
	Liaison with parents (including telephone contact time)
	Conduct a final evaluation

column of the table. Completing this table helps leaders and others to recognise the time required to put a group programme into operation, and it is useful when making decisions regarding programme dates. It is also helpful in time management, as it enables workers to schedule into their workload sufficient time to complete the necessary tasks. Such a timetable can be useful when submitting proposals for funding and resourcing group programmes. It also provides a visual guide and check list of the sequence of tasks to be completed.

Planning the overall programme and individual sessions

Chapter 5 describes the steps to follow when planning an overall programme and individual sessions within that programme. The type of group and theoretical model to be used will influence the overall and individual session format.

Important issues to consider at the planning stage include group size and composition.

Group size

Larger groups are often more economic but risk dilution of attention to individual needs and may lack the development of cohesion. It is important not to compromise the needs of children by running a group that is too large.

There is no general rule regarding group size, because this will depend on the goals of the programme, the age of the children, degree of acting out, manifestation of disturbance and the activities which are planned. It is fairly difficult to work with fewer than four children in a group, because with only three children there may be joining between two of the children to the exclusion of the other.

Rose and Edleson (1987), referring to therapy groups, suggest that groups usually range in size from three to eight members, as groups larger than eight make it difficult to permit every member to get their personal needs met in each session. Schnitzer de Neuhaus (1985) believes there is considerable agreement regarding an optimal size of five to seven children for therapy groups, depending on the group's composition. Moreover, she recommends a maximum of six children if there is only one group facilitator, and only four or five if the children are very active, aggressive or hostile. However, she points out that if attendance problems are extreme, eight or nine children may need to be included to ensure five or six are usually present.

For young children aged nine years or below, small groups are usually preferable. Children in this age group are not able to rely on peer interactions as easily as older children. Predictably with children of six or seven years the major source of communication, both verbal and non-verbal, is generally with the leaders. Certainly they require a significant amount of individual attention from leaders. Six to eight children is generally a suitable size for such groups. With children of this age, too large a group may create an environment that is over-stimulating and confusing for them. In contrast, small groups are more comfortable and safer with the result that they are usually more able to gain mastery over their own issues as well as those presented by the group.

For older age groups, from ten years onwards and into adolescence, suitable group sizes may be from eight to twelve participants, depending on the purpose of the group.

When deciding how many children to include in a group, it should be remembered that there is often a natural attrition with some children dropping out either from individual sessions, or from the whole programme. Dropping out may occur because children are uninterested in the group programme, feel threatened by it, are affected by illness, move away, have parents who are either unhappy with the programme or have difficulty in bringing the child to the group.

Group size should be limited if there is only one facilitator. With two facilitators, it is possible to work with a larger number of children.

Group composition

Group composition must take account of age, gender, culture, purpose of the group and level of activity.

For younger children an age spread of only one to two years is preferable, whereas for latency age children and young adolescents a spread of three years is generally satisfactory. It is more important to consider a child's developmental age than chronological age with regard to this spread, and to take into account maturity and social adjustment.

For many groups, it is preferable to have balance in a group rather than a completely homogenous group. Balance is achieved by taking into account the various physical, emotional, psychological, socio-economic, personality characteristics and attributes of potential group members. This creates a dynamic and flexible group climate where tensions and differences can exist throughout the programme. A balance is also useful in promoting self-regulation of behaviours (Schnitzer de Neuhaus, 1985). Various studies on successful groups have shown that the right mix of members ensures group efficiency and productivity (Wheelan, 1994).

Whenever possible and appropriate we prefer to have groups of mixed gender, because these groups tend to be more productive than same gender groups. However, it is not always appropriate to have a mixed gender group. For example, it would not usually be sensible to include both sexes in groups dealing with sexual abuse or sexual offending issues.

It should be expected that with mixed groups of latency age children, the group will divide into boy–girl subgroups very quickly, with communication predominantly between same-sex groups. However, this should not preclude the achievement of useful goals in an environment similar to the wider world. The problems that arise can be addressed in the group and represent a valuable learning experience (Rose and Edleson, 1987).

In local communities where the population is racially and ethnically mixed, it is generally preferable to have groups that reflect the balance in that community. Rose and Edleson (1987) found that relationships between racial groups improved significantly over time where groups were mixed, but caution that they did not use a control group in their research. Where there are racial or ethnic minorities, it is recommended that at least two representatives from the minority population be included in a group. To include only one representative might have serious consequences with that member being scapegoated. In schools or community environments where racial tensions are high or where problems are peculiar to a particular racial group, it may be more appropriate to have racially homogenous groups.

Planning the intake procedure

When planning an intake procedure, decisions need to be made about the selection of children for inclusion in a group. Both inclusion and exclusion criteria need to be established and leaders need to decide on a process for the selection of suitable children (see Chapter 6).

Planning and organising the practical arrangements

Planning and organising the practical arrangements involves booking the venue, purchasing any materials required, arranging for the loan or hiring of equipment and making arrangements for presenters or guest speakers.

Materials to be purchased might include art materials, video tapes, cooking materials and equipment for use in motor activities such as bats and balls. Equipment to be hired might include items such as a VCR and monitor, computer games or a video camera.

Sometimes in a programme it is useful to invite a guest speaker who has expertise in a particular subject. Such speakers need to be booked in advance. For example, in a psycho-educational group looking at sexual issues, an expert speaker on HIV or sexually transmitted diseases generally might be invited.

Some group programmes require visits to sites away from the group room. For example, a developmental group may wish to practise living skills such as travelling by public transport or attending a matinee performance. Leaders need to check that the proposed activity is possible on the planned dates.

Preparing and organising advertising

There are some groups that require no advertising. These are groups where all the children belong to a particular system (for example a school) where workers have identified them as belonging to a particular target group. Such children may be informally invited to participate in an assessment process to determine individual suitability for group membership. Additionally, there are those children in systems specifically designed to accommodate children from particular target groups. For example, a group may be set up for children who are inpatients in a psychiatric ward of a children's hospital or in a group home.

Many children's groups do need to be advertised to enable information about the group to reach parents and children who are not known to the leaders. Additionally, advertising can help children and their parents to make an informed choice about whether or not the child should join the group.

Advertising may include:

- A description of children who are likely to benefit from the group
- The age range
- Objectives of the group
- The group programme
- Location
- Cost of participation
- Dates
- Times
- Information about the leaders and the sponsoring agency
- A map showing the location of the venue
- Information about public transport and/or parking
- Information about childminding facilities (if these will be available for siblings)

- A closing date for enquiries from interested parents
- A contact phone number for those who are interested

When advertising, leaders need to take account of the time needed to receive replies and to meet with parents and their children to assess suitability (see Chapter 6).

Organising and carrying out an intake procedure

For those groups where advertising is used, an intake procedure is needed as a screening process so that potentially suitable children can be invited to participate in an assessment process. The screening process will also eliminate those children who clearly do not fit the criteria for group membership. The process of organising and carrying out an intake procedure is described in Chapter 6.

While planning, leaders should decide on a cutoff date after which applications for group membership will not be accepted.

Assessment of possible group members

The assessment of children with regard to suitability for inclusion in a group is described in Chapter 6. Adequate time needs to be allocated for this process.

Notifying successful and unsuccessful applicants

This is discussed in Chapter 6. Adequate time needs to be allocated for this task so that parents or carers of children who are assessed as unsuitable can be informed in a way that is not damaging and encouraged to explore other options.

Supervisor and leader/s meetings

Time should be allocated for a number of meetings between the leaders and their professional supervisors. Such meetings should be scheduled at regular intervals throughout all stages of the programme from the time of initial planning to the time of final evaluation after conclusion of the programme.

Supervision should focus on improving practice, on the relationship between the two leaders, if there are two, and on personal issues of leaders that arise as a consequence of leading the group. Supervision should also address the roles leaders take in each group session (see Chapter 7).

Preparation before individual sessions

The most important part of preparing for a session is for the leaders to attend to their own emotional states so they can disengage from distracting and intruding personal and work related issues. Where there are two leaders, they also need to connect with each other and share relevant information that might influence their working relationship or practical running of the group.

Preparation needs to involve leaders familiarising themselves with the programme for the day. On examining the planned programme, they should consider possible modifications to the programme. These modifications may need to be made as a consequence of feedback or of the leaders' observations of behaviours and processes from previous sessions which have been unhelpful in achieving goals. Leaders also need to give consideration to, and agree on, the management of individual member's behaviours which might be anticipated in the group as a result of the programme and/or process.

Practical arrangements, including setting up the room, preparing a snack if this is included and checking equipment is available and works, need to be carried out so that they are completed before group members arrive.

Running group sessions

Careful planning of each session, as described in Chapter 5, will enable leaders to have some confidence that groups can start and finish at the designated times. The leaders' role in running group sessions is described in Chapter 7.

Clearing up and debriefing after each session

Adequate time needs to be allocated for clearing up, particularly in groups where materials, equipment and activity are used. If the venue is hired, time may be needed to restore the group room to its initial condition.

It is essential that leaders allow time to debrief with each other and/or with their supervisor after each session (see Chapter 7).

Liaison with parents

It is difficult, if not impossible, to estimate the time needed to liaise with parents. Wherever possible, time should be made to meet with parents privately or to have contact out of group time. Parents will frequently want to talk to a leader immediately after a group session, but this is often not suitable because leaders need to clear up and debrief. However, leaders do need to be flexible in attending to parents', carers' and children's needs, and sometimes should pass on information immediately after a session to help a child move back comfortably into his or her own environment.

Conducting a final evaluation

Time needs to be set aside for evaluating the outcomes of group programmes (see Chapter 9).

5 Designing a group programme

It can be both useful and satisfying for group leaders to design programmes to meet the needs of a particular target group. When designing a programme leaders may wish to use the process described in this chapter. In this process, leaders start by developing an overall programme and then design specific programmes for each individual session. It is advantageous to develop the overall programme first rather than starting by designing the individual session programmes. By doing this the overall programme is more likely to grow from, and be directly connected with, the relevant theory and research. Additionally, the overall programme is more likely to be consistently geared towards meeting the children's needs.

The process described for designing a group programme is equally suitable for planning topic-focused groups or system-based groups.

OVERALL PROGRAMME DESIGN

To demonstrate the process used in designing an overall programme a specific target group will be used as an example. The example selected involves children aged nine to twelve years who have witnessed violence at home. The steps required in designing a programme are illustrated in Figure 5.1. Each step listed in the figure will now be described.

Listing assumptions about the target group

As discussed in Chapter 3, leaders need to fully research the relevant literature relating to the target group so that they are familiar with current theory and research findings. They also need to take into account information from their own experiences in relation to the target group, and information provided by other workers who have

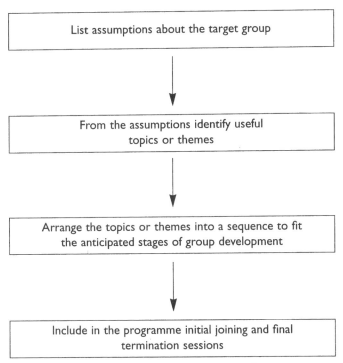

Figure 5.1   Plan for the overall design of a group programme

had experience in working with a similar group. Leaders are then in a position to brainstorm and list realistic and relevant assumptions about the children concerned.

For the example chosen, children who come from families where violence has occurred in the home, a list of assumptions is provided in Chapter 3.

Identifying useful topics or themes

Leaders must take account of the developmental level of the children who are to be involved in a group. This is essential because, as discussed previously, a group programme must be able to address the children's issues at their developmental level. Having listed assumptions and taken into account developmental level, leaders are then in a position to identify topics and/or themes to be used in the programme.

Let us consider planning a group for children from violent families. By examining the list of assumptions we have made about these children

Table 5.1   Developing topics and themes from assumptions

Assumptions	Topic or theme for a group programme
They may have intrusive thoughts, experience survivor guilt, and lack validation of their experiences	Sharing experiences
They may have issues around family secrets, power and control, and shame and embarassment	Breaking the secret and talking about abuse
They may have difficulty in understanding who is responsible for violence, and confusion about gender roles and attributes	Attributing responsibility of parental violence to the adult/s involved
They may have confusion about whether abuse is okay or not, and continue abuse patterns in their own lives	Understanding that abuse is not okay under any circumstances
They may have distorted values regarding violence in society	Defining abuse and violence
They may have anxiety about their own safety	Feeling safe and having fun
They may have poor social skills, poor impulse control, and poor problem solving skills (so they may use violence as a problem solving technique in school and with peers and family)	Understanding that it is okay to be angry and learning how to ask to get needs met without being aggressive

we may decide that important topics or themes for the group programme might be those listed in Table 5.1.

In any programme of limited duration it may be necessary to select from the full list of assumptions and only to use the most relevant for the particular children concerned.

Arranging topics or themes into a sequence

Each topic or theme may be suitable for one or more sessions of the group programme. There may be too many topics or themes for all of them to be included in the programme because of time limitations. In this case, either some topics or themes need to be combined, or a decision needs to be made as to which are the most important ones to include. Leaders need to be aware that if they try to cover too much material the information may become fragmented and diluted, resulting in the group experience not having as much impact on members.

The overall programme should take account of the stages of group formation, as described in Chapter 7, so that the topics or themes used in each session are compatible with those stages. For example, the topics and themes listed in Table 5.1 might be re-arranged into the following order so they fit with the anticipated stages of group development and follow a sensible and logical sequence, effectively building on each other:

1. Defining abuse and violence
2. Breaking the secret and talking about abuse
3. Sharing experiences
4. Understanding that abuse is not okay under any circumstances
5. Understanding that it is okay to be angry and learning how to ask to get needs met without being aggressive
6. Attributing responsibility of parental violence to the adult/s involved
7. Feeling safe and having fun

The first topic lends itself to a didactic approach and does not necessarily demand personal sharing. It is therefore appropriately placed at the beginning of the programme when the group is in the initial stage of group development (the 'forming' stage). By comparison, the second, third and fourth topics progressively invite more self-disclosure and fit with the 'storming' stage where there is opportunity for the processing of group interactions and behaviours. Topics five, six and seven are best used in the 'norming' stage when the group is more cohesive and supportive and is able to focus on productive work which might involve making changes in thinking and behaviours.

Including joining and termination sessions

The programmes for the first and last sessions of a series of sessions are particularly important. For most children joining a group is a significant event which may be stressful and anxiety provoking. It is therefore useful to include a first session where the focus is on joining rather than on a particular topic. Similarly, the last session of a group programme should focus on separation. This can be done by using activities that tend to emphasise separation and individuality rather than promoting cohesion.

For some groups, it may be useful to start with an initial session involving only parents or carers and not their children. This enables parents or carers to deal with any anxieties they may have in connection with their children joining the group. Parents or carers can also be fully informed about the group programme and its goals. As a consequence they are more likely to be supportive of their children attending the group, to understand their children's responses to particular parts of the programme and to be supportive of behaviour changes and attitudes promoted through group participation.

Consider again the example of a group programme for children from families where violence has occurred. If an initial session for parents is included, followed by a joining session for the children, and a termination session is added at the end of the programme, the sequence and titles of sessions become:

Session 1: Parent information group
Session 2: Joining and getting to know you
Session 3: Defining abuse and violence
Session 4: Breaking the secret and talking about abuse
Session 5: Sharing experiences
Session 6: Understanding abuse is not okay under any circumstances
Session 7: Understanding that it is okay to be angry and learning how to ask to get needs met without being aggressive
Session 8: Attributing responsibility of parental violence to the adult/s involved
Session 9: Feeling safe and having fun
Session 10: Closure

INDIVIDUAL SESSION DESIGN

Figure 5.2 illustrates a process which can be used when planning the content and programmes for individual group sessions. Each session needs to have clearly defined goals. The achievement of these goals is then dependent on interventions from the theoretical framework to be used and also, for many groups, on the use of activities.

Group sessions that make use of activities work best when they include variety. This is conducive to continued interest and allows group energy to rise and fall so that the children become neither exhausted nor bored. Thus the activities used should vary so that they are at times fun, serious, messy, clean, relaxing, risky, energetic, easy to do, challenging, familiar, new, quiet or noisy. Sometimes the activities may involve sitting quietly and at other times they may involve movement.

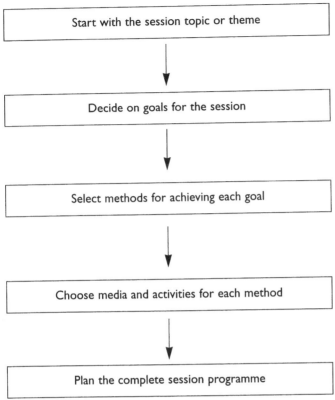

Figure 5.2   Plan for designing the programme for a single group session

Often, in groups for young children, interest and ability to concentrate is limited to ten or fifteen minutes when focusing on issues or topics that are difficult or challenging. For less demanding activities, which are enjoyable, young children are generally able to show interest for longer periods.

A programme which includes a variety of activities, each lasting for about ten to fifteen minutes, will usually keep children involved, connected and focused. Of course this will vary according to age. For example, adolescents spend much of their time in discussion and are pre-disposed to self-disclosure (Rose, S.R., 1998). Consequently they can be involved in extended practice activities such as sophisticated role playing strategies with scenarios which might involve the whole group.

It is sensible to design each session so that the programme flows smoothly from one activity to another and maintains interest and energy while continuing to address the relevant theme or topic.

Continually referring back to the theme or topic for the session helps to 'tie' the programme together so that it flows naturally from one activity to another.

The first session needs to address the children's needs and anxieties associated with joining a new group. Towards the end of a programme the children need to be prepared for the termination of group sessions. The last session must deal with issues related to closure and the loss of the group.

Deciding on goals for the session

It is essential for leaders to set clear goals for each session so the group does not deteriorate into a purposeless group and so that outcomes can be evaluated with regard to these goals (see Chapter 9 with regard to evaluation).

As described previously, in planning the overall programme for a target group topics or themes are identified for each session. These are then used to help leaders decide on goals for each session.

The goals should describe what the leaders hope to achieve during that session. For example, consider designing a session programme for children from families where there has been violence, using the topic, 'breaking the secret'. Possible goals to be achieved in the session might be to:

1. Enable the children to talk about their families and the violence in them.
2. Help the children share their own personal experiences of violence.
3. Help the children to feel as though they are not alone.

The chosen topic for another week in the same programme might be, 'sharing experiences'. In this session a list of goals to fit the topic might be:

1. Encourage the children to discuss personal experiences of family violence.
2. Discover and identify the triggers of their anxiety.
3. Explore different responses to anxiety reactions after overwhelming experiences.

Selecting methods for achieving goals

Once goals have been set, leaders need to decide how they intend to achieve them. There are several methods they might use. For example, the children might be asked to work in any of the following ways:

- In the whole group
- In a sub-group
- As part of a team
- In pairs
- Individually

There may be advantages to working in a variety of these ways during a group session depending on the activities used at various times and the goals to be achieved. When working in the whole group members have a greater sense of belonging, more opportunity for vicarious learning and, depending on the stage of group development, a greater opportunity for catharsis from personal sharing. Whole group work also provides an optimal environment for discussing common needs of members and this may be helpful for normalising and de-stigmatisation.

In sub-groups there is a greater opportunity for personal sharing and more intense and in-depth exchange of ideas and opinions. Tasks may be easier or more difficult to accomplish because individual differences tend to be highlighted in a small group. However, the environment may be safer for the practice of new behaviours.

Team work provides a good environment for children to practise and experience different roles such as leader, helper, observer, worker or instructor. It provides an opportunity to experience competition and the impact of winning, losing, collaborating and cooperating. Behaviour which does not serve the best interests of the team is more likely to occur overtly and be observed. This provides opportunity for processing and learning.

Children working in pairs experience the difficulties and benefits of interpersonal relationships in a one-to-one situation. The alliance with one other person may subsequently make it easy for a child to re-join a whole group activity.

Working individually can give children the opportunity to focus and connect with their own personal thoughts and feelings. They may discover personal strengths and be able to share or compare their own abilities with those of others.

While working individually or in any of the above groupings, leaders might choose to use discussion, a cognitive activity, a creative activity, motor activity, role play, an educational or a projective activity. Some activities are more useful in achieving particular goals than others. For example, cognitive activities will lend themselves more to problem solving and solution focused goals, role plays may focus on the experience of interpersonal relationships, creative and projective activities facilitate self-disclosure and personal sharing, discussion relies heavily on communication skills and understanding what others are saying, and educational activities are important for imparting new information. Motor activities provide an outlet for energy and the opportunity to use social relationship skills.

Choosing media and activities

Children spend significant parts of their lives in play and related activities, which are usually enjoyable and sometimes fun. Because they spend so much time in this way, many of their perceptions of themselves and of the world around them derive from play-related activities. It therefore makes sense to use play and activity to join with children and to engage them in processes involving change.

When counselling children individually we make use of media and activity in conjunction with counselling skills to help children communicate openly with us and promote change. The processes used are described in the books, *Counselling Children* (Geldard and Geldard, 1997) and *Counselling Adolescents* (Geldard and Geldard, 1999). The same approach can be used when working with children in groups. Certainly play and activity are very important tools for working with groups of younger children. Group leaders need to develop knowledge and skills in order to use these instruments to assist children in learning to cooperate with others, to negotiate conflicts and to take others into account. It is not the game, activity or outcome that is important but rather the processing of resulting behaviours and emotions. The processing of an activity, as described in Chapter 8, is an essential part of any group method for achieving goals. Through processing, experiences may be shared, feelings addressed and new ways of thinking and behaving developed. Processing also provides an opportunity for the use of educational input.

Malekoff (1997) describes activity as more than a 'tool', more than programmed content, more than 'canned' exercises and more than a mechanistic means to an end. In addition to structured games and exercises, he points out that activity may be spontaneously created by a group of young people. He suggests that activity promotes a sense of competence, a sense of belonging, self-discovery, invention and creativity.

Rose, S.D. (1998) strongly supports the use of activities and games when running groups for young people, believing that activities provide conditions in which concrete skills can be informally practised and reinforced in a way that is more realistic than role playing. Activities provide the opportunity for self-growth, improving interpersonal relationships and learning.

Reference to the work of the authors discussed above strongly supports the view that the use of media and activities are of considerable value in group programmes for children. Clearly for many groups it can be advantageous to make use of media and activity when selecting methods for the achievement of goals. Leaders do need to remember, however, that the processes, tasks and activities selected and used to help individual members change and grow in a group depend on the theoretical beliefs relevant to that group (Wheelan, 1994).

Useful media and activities

The range of media which can be used when running groups for children is limitless. Commonly used media and activities include:

art materials	games	work-sheets	puppets
miniature animals	video tapes	craft	role play
clay	puzzles	construction	free play

Planning a complete session programme

Chapters 10, 11, 12, and 13 include sample programmes for particular target groups. These demonstrate the way in which programmes for individual sessions can be structured and varied.

When designing a session programme, the template shown in Figure 5.3 may be useful. Activities are entered on the template to indicate

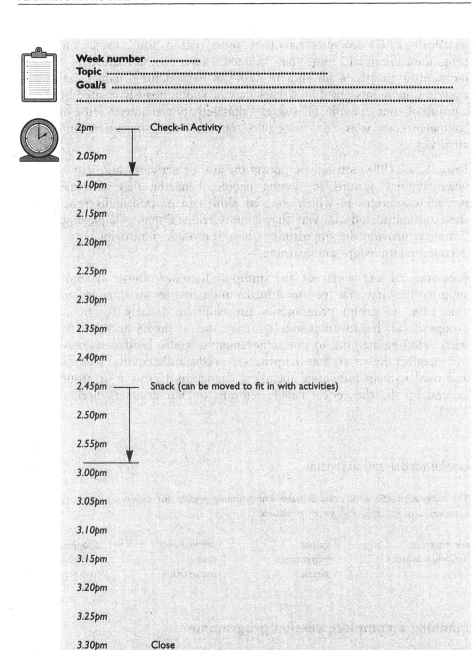

Week number ....
Topic ....
Goal/s ....
....

2pm	——	Check-in Activity
2.05pm		
2.10pm		
2.15pm		
2.20pm		
2.25pm		
2.30pm		
2.35pm		
2.40pm		
2.45pm	——	Snack (can be moved to fit in with activities)
2.50pm		
2.55pm		
3.00pm		
3.05pm		
3.10pm		
3.15pm		
3.20pm		
3.25pm		
3.30pm		Close

Materials needed ....
....

Figure 5.3   Weekly session template

the time when the activity is likely to begin, with an arrow used to indicate suggested duration.

As an example, consider the structures of the individual session programmes included in the group programme for children from families where violence has occurred (see Chapter 10). It should be noted that the programme for each session starts with a joining and/or check-in activity. This is recommended to help the children deal with a whole range of feelings, anxieties and different energy levels, and to allow a feeling of well-being to develop. For similar reasons, Silveira and Trafford (1988) suggest starting each session with a warm-up exercise. This can be an alternative to using a joining or check-in activity; deciding which to use will depend on the type and purpose of the group.

Each session in the sample session programme (Chapter 10) includes snack time. When running groups, this is clearly optional. However, including a snack time can be particularly useful for groups of long duration as it provides a break, some food (especially useful for after school groups) and enables the children to relax together in an unstructured way. Sometimes leaders will notice behaviours during a snack time which may not occur during the main session programme. It may then be helpful to process these behaviours in the whole group when the session re-starts.

To illustrate how a variety of methods and activities can be used to achieve goals, consider session five of the sample programme in Chapter 10. The topic for the session is 'Sharing experiences'. Goals which the leaders hope to achieve are to:

1. Help the group share personal and family experiences related to violence.
2. Enable the group to experience the accompanying feelings.
3. Help the children discover that other children in the group have also experienced violence in the home.
4. Enable the children to feel less different and less ashamed of their own families.

Table 5.2 illustrates how the programme varies in the use of method and activity while maintaining a focus likely to result in the achievement of the goals. It will be noticed that in the session there is an emphasis on whole group work, appropriate for the stage of group development because it is anticipated that by session five the group will be cohesive and mutually supportive.

Table 5.2   Illustration of variations within a session programme

The programme (for session 5 of the sample programme given in Chapter 10)	Method	Activity/media
The initial check-in activity helps the children to re-connect with each other, to put aside intrusive emotional feelings and thoughts which might interfere with the group's focus.	Discussion in the whole group	Weather chart
The children are invited to use art to paint or draw their worst experience either symbolically or representationally. This provides an opportunity for the children to get in touch with and express feelings that are tied to traumatic experiences.	Creative individual activity	Art
The previous activity is processed to explore whether memories of unpleasant experiences intrude at times, and to discover how the memories make the children feel now. During processing the children are supported and encouraged to share.	Whole group discussion	The children's art work
The children play the game, 'Sardines' so that previous intense activity is followed by an activity which allows for release through movement.	Whole group motor activity	A game
The previous activity is processed in terms of secrecy and can be likened to the secrecy of family violence. Discussion of how that secrecy can be broken can follow.	Whole group discussion	None
The activity, 'What hands can do', provides an opportunity for the children to share personal experiences of helpful and unhelpful events in their lives. Working in pairs is mutually supportive and less threatening than sharing in the whole group. Those who were unable to share in the whole group may now be able to talk to a partner.	Collaborative activity in pairs	The activity, 'What hands can do'
The session's activities are processed to allow children to re-join with the whole group, to give affirmations and support with regard to personal sharing, and enables the children to tie together the things learnt in the session.	Whole group discussion	None
A snack is provided to make closure easier	Whole group	Food

Putting the session plan into action

Sometimes it is useful to talk to a group at the beginning of each session about the planned programme for that session. While a group session is running leaders need to be constantly aware of the group's responses to the programme. These responses need to be processed as described in Chapter 8. Also, the programme may need to be adapted while it is running to meet the current needs of the group. Session programmes should not be used rigidly, but as guides that can be modified to meet the 'here and now' needs of the group. For example, if the energy in a group is dropping, rather than continue by doing a quiet activity as scheduled in the programme, the leaders might move the group into an energising game which requires physical movement and is fun. By deviating from the previously devised plan, the group can become energised and then return to the quiet activity previously scheduled.

After each session, the programme needs to be reviewed and evaluated, so that the following session's programme can be amended, if necessary, to take into account information from the session just ended. Feedback from group members can be useful in this process (see Chapter 9).

PART III

RUNNING A GROUP PROGRAMME

6 Assessment of children for inclusion in a group programme

Chapter 3 discussed the importance of identifying and selecting a suitable target group of children with similar needs. It was emphasised that in most cases these needs will be dependent not only on the child's particular experiences, but also on the child's developmental age. Because of this, it is usually wise to ensure that the children in a group are all of similar developmental age. There are some exceptions to this; for example, for systems groups or when dealing with groups of siblings there may be advantages in including children of differing developmental age.

Once leaders have identified the needs of a particular target group, they can formulate appropriate goals and be clear about the purpose of running a programme to suit this group. They are then in a position to be able to develop a suitable programme. After a programme has been developed, an assessment process needs to be devised to decide which children are suitable for inclusion in the group programme and which are not.

THE PURPOSE OF ASSESSMENT

There is a view that, at best, selecting group members may be 'guess work' (Henry, 1992). However, experience suggests that by looking at specific factors in composing children's groups it is possible to avoid a catastrophe, a dysfunctional group or at least a major conflict that may prove destructive to the group (Fatout, 1996). Additionally, the use of screening interviews with children will diminish the prospect of children dropping out (Soo, 1996).

An assessment process is useful for:

- Establishing rapport with the child, and parents or carers
- Determining whether the child's needs match the identified needs of the target group
- Determining whether the child will be able to function in a group
- Determining whether the child will be likely to benefit from the planned group programme
- Determining whether the child's inclusion will lead to the formation of a group of balanced or compatible composition
- Obtaining information which will be useful for evaluating the effectiveness of a programme and changes in individual children

Establishing rapport

An assessment process provides an opportunity for children to meet with leaders before making a decision about whether to join a group or not. In the same way that leaders need to decide who to include, the children themselves need to feel comfortable with prospective leaders. During assessment, leaders and children become acquainted at some level. The children have an opportunity to ask questions about the group and its composition, and to understand the leaders' expectations of group behaviour. Leaders can give children information concerning the purpose, style and activities of the group as well as practical details such as duration, time, place and length of sessions.

Parents and carers often worry about whether or not to arrange for their children to join a group. They may worry about who the group leaders are, what their qualifications are, what their management style will be and whether their children will be safe in the group. They may be concerned about information their child might reveal in the group contex and may be anxious in case their children will be negatively influenced by other children in the group. In order for parents and carers to feel comfortable with their children joining a group, they need to have an opportunity to meet with leaders and to talk through their concerns. By doing this they can gain confidence and trust in the leaders' ability to provide a safe and useful group environment. Parents also need to be able to talk to leaders about the group and its purpose.

A major issue for parents and carers is often related to confidentiality. Leaders therefore need to have a clear policy about confidentiality and to be open in discussing this (see Chapter 8).

Do the child's needs match the target group's?

Determining whether the child's needs match the needs of the target group is clearly important for a group to be maximally effective, both for the individual child and for the group as a whole. Sometimes it can be advantageous to include a balance of children. Thus a child whose needs match some of the needs of the target group, but not all, might be included. Each child will have a unique way of responding to past experiences and present situations and will have individual coping strategies. Including children who have different personal resources, experiences and behaviours may have a positive influence on the way a group functions. Additionally, their inclusion may result in the generation of useful material that can be processed to the benefit of the group. It is important, however, when including children not to compromise the goals of a group with the intention of providing balance in the attributes of group members.

Will the child function in the group?

Assessing whether a child will be able to function in a group involves answering two questions:

1. Does the child have the necessary skills to cope in a group?
2. Will the child be able to fit in with other group members?

An assessment needs to be made of each child's physical, emotional and psychological resources to determine whether these are likely to be adequate in enabling the child to cope. The child's ability to fit in will depend on her or his behavioural responses when relating with others. An individual child's ability to fit in with other group members is desirable in order to achieve group cohesion. Generally, if the child does not have the necessary skills, the programme may be compromised and the child is unlikely to benefit. However, there are exceptions to this. Groups are often used to enable children develop skills in handling negative experiences such as frustration, teasing, inappropriate social advances from other children and issues around inclusion and exclusion. Groups may also be used to help children learn to replace maladaptive social behaviours with adaptive ones. Consequently, selection criteria for some groups will result in children who do have difficulty in fitting in with others being included, provided that the leaders believe group processes can be used with these children to promote the required changes.

For most groups an attempt should be made to select group members who are not likely to impede group processes and whose well-being will not be jeopardised by the group experience. Some children may not have the required ego strength to join some groups without being damaged. They need to be excluded and other provisions made for helping them. Additionally, some children who are being assessed for inclusion in psychotherapy groups may need to be excluded because their behaviour is so bizarre that it will frighten other children, or might be personally or culturally unacceptable to them (Rose and Edleson, 1987).

In assessing children for inclusion in a group, leaders need to be clear about the goals of the programme and to recognise what is developmentally appropriate behaviour for children within the proposed target group.

Will the child benefit from the programme?

If a child's needs match the needs of the target group, we can expect the child to benefit from the group programme because this will have been specifically designed to meet the identified needs. However, there are exceptions. We need to look at the possibility that there may be influences in the child's life, or particular characteristics of the child, which will interfere with the child's ability to benefit from a particular programme.

Consider a situation where a child's parent/s, carer/s or siblings have negative attitudes with regard to the child's participation in a group. In this case the child may become confused and/or stressed by participation in the group. Instead of benefiting, the child may find the group experience unhelpful.

Some children may be unable to benefit from a group programme because they have very low ego strength, have excessively high levels of acting out behaviour or are unable to maintain their attention for even short periods of time in a group situation.

Balance and compatibility requirements of the group

One of the purposes of assessment is to enable leaders to discover differences and similarities between children so that a group of balanced composition can be created (see Chapter 4).

Evaluating effectiveness

In Chapter 9 we will discuss the evaluation of the outcomes of group work. One way of evaluating outcomes is to take pre- and post-measures of variables which will change over the life of the group if group goals are met. At the time when leaders are planning the initial assessment they also need to decide on the evaluation process. Before the group starts it may be necessary to collect specific data relating to the children who are selected to join the group so that this data can be used in the evaluation process. The time of assessment provides a convenient opportunity for the collection of such data.

THE ASSESSMENT PROCESS

Careful programme planning followed by an effective assessment procedure is essential to ensure a successful group experience with the achievement of identified goals. Outcomes may be severely compromised if the assessment process does not carefully tease out important factors that need to be identified. Figure 6.1 provides an over-view of an assessment process.

The assessment process needs to be respectful of the rights of the child as well as those of the parent/s or carer/s. The child and parent/s or carer/s need to be informed of the purpose of the assessment process. It is recommended that they should be told that it will be a two-way process, where both the needs of the child and family and the needs of the leaders will be respected and met. Thus the leaders will make a decision about whether or not to include the child in the group, and the child and family will be provided with the necessary information to enable them to make a decision regarding participation by the child. The child and parent/s or carer/s need to feel free to make a decision that the child will not join the group, if that is their preferred choice. Children who are made to join a group against their wishes, or who are confused about why they are in a group, or whose parent/s or carer/s do not wish them to be in a group, are unlikely to gain from participation and unlikely to contribute positively to the group process.

The first prerequisite of a group programme is obtaining an adequate number of potential members (Rose and Edleson, 1987). A recruitment campaign is an essential part of many group programmes so that a large enough number of people are made aware of the

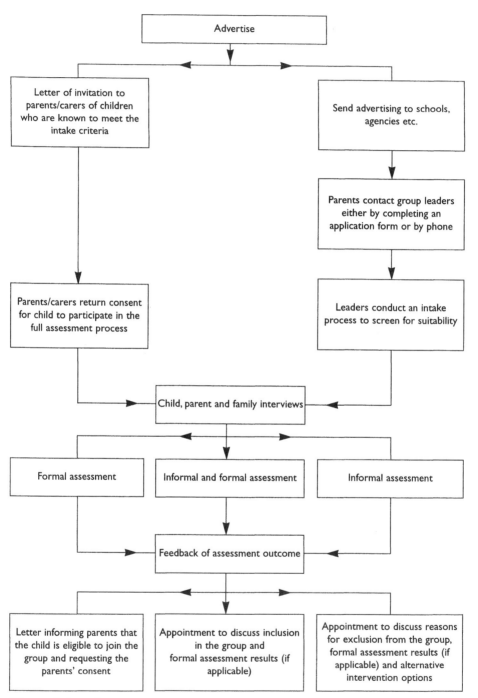

Figure 6.1   An assessment process

programme, its goals and other practical considerations. Advertising may be sent to possible referral sources such as agencies, parents, teachers or counsellors. Advertising can be carried out through the use of letters, fliers, posters, phone calls and radio or television announcements.

The intake procedure

As discussed in Chapter 4, for those groups where advertising is used an intake procedure is needed as a screening process so that children who may be suitable can be invited to participate in a more complete assessment process. The screening process eliminates those who clearly do not fit the criteria for group membership and do not warrant further assessment.

During an intake procedure, suitability is determined by making use of inclusion and exclusion criteria. If, for example, we consider a group for children between the ages of nine and twelve years with Attention Deficit Hyperactivity Disorder, one inclusion criteria might be that only those children who are currently having their disorder managed with the use of medication be considered for inclusion. Also, children who are unable to read or write might be excluded if the programme is to rely heavily on literacy skills.

It is important that inclusion and exclusion criteria are sufficiently broad to allow for the inclusion of children who have a variety of personality characteristics and behaviours (see Chapter 4). Generally, the most effective groups have a balanced composition, so that there is some variation in the performance or behavioural characteristics of members. This variation can be useful as it is likely to promote lively interaction (Bertcher and Maple, 1985).

Identified needs and personal resources are of primary importance when selecting children for inclusion in a group. Issues relating to age, gender, behaviours and culture and ethnicity also need to be assessed to confirm that they will enable the child to gain from the group programme. Where groups contain children of mixed ethnicity it may, depending on the purpose of the group, be desirable to include several members from each ethnic group so that individuals from each group receive appropriate peer support. With regard to these personal attributes, it needs to be remembered that some children may be more suited to individual work than group work. Care needs to be taken to ensure those who are different are not excluded merely because of difference. However, exclusion from a group is usually sensible where there are significant differences between the needs of the individual and the identified needs of the target group.

The intake process

Generally, after reading advertising material interested parents or carers will contact the leaders. Leaders therefore need to have a checklist relating to inclusion and exclusion criteria to help them determine whether a thorough assessment of the child for possible inclusion is warranted. By using a checklist decisions are more likely to be made on an informed rather than a subjective and/or ad hoc basis.

At this stage, parents or carers of those children who do not meet the inclusion criteria need to be informed of the reasons why their child does not fit into the proposed group. Additionally, they need to be helped to explore alternative options for their child. To help leaders in this process a resources list of alternative services for children should be available so that relevant information can be passed on to interested parents or carers. Exclusion of children from a group may suggest that a different kind of group would be useful in meeting the needs of some of those who have been excluded. Alternatively, these children may be able to benefit from individual help. It needs to be recognised that an exclusion criterion for one type of group might be an inclusion criteria for another type of group. For example, a child who has difficulty with turn-taking behaviour might be excluded from some types of group but might meet the inclusion criteria for a social skills group, where the undesirable behaviour will be specifically addressed.

In some situations leaders do not personally have choice over which children are to be included. Thus they may find that personal issues for them arise in connection with the inclusion of certain children in the group. If this occurs, it is sensible to address these issues by talking with an independent supervisor.

Where, at the intake stage, children, as described by their parents or others, match broad inclusion criteria and do not fit exclusion criteria, an appointment needs to be arranged to enable a full assessment of the child's suitability for inclusion in the group.

The assessment interview

Assessment interviews provide an opportunity for leaders to judge a child's motivation and capacity to engage in a group programme, to judge the parents' or carers' ability to be supportive of the child's participation in the group, to obtain a diagnostic impression of the child where appropriate and to explain to parents or carers and the child the purpose and style of the group. Additionally, the assessment process provides an opportunity for leaders to begin a relationship with the child so that entry into the group is easier (Schnitzer de Neuhaus, 1985).

It is respectful for parent/s or carer/s and the child to be fully informed about the purpose and style of the assessment. Having introduced themselves, for example, the leaders may tell the family that the assessment consists of one session where some of the time is spent with the child, some with the parents or carers and the rest of the time with the whole family. The purpose of the assessment may be described in terms of 'getting to know each other' and coming to a decision together about whether a group programme will be useful for the child. The leaders' expectations of children who might join the group should be explained at this time, and any questions that the parent/s or carer/s and/or child might have should be answered.

Leaders need to view children as children, not as diminutive adults. They need to recognise that their expectations need to be commensurate with the children's development. However, even though they are not adults, children can be very knowledgeable about themselves. They can be expected to make age appropriate decisions (Siepker and Kandaras, 1985). Their decisions need to be respected, particularly with regard to participation in a group. Leaders must take care not to tempt or coerce children into making decisions to join a group if that is not what they want to do.

Assessment can be carried out informally, formally or using a combination of both.

Informal assessment of the child

Informal assessment of the child relies on clinical observation. Often such assessment will be carried out partly in the presence of the parent/s or carer/s and partly with the child, either individually or in a group. Assessing the child by observing him or her in a group setting has some advantages over individual assessment. It allows direct observation of, and focused attention on, vital aspects of functioning such as peer relations, social competency and how the child deals with his or her anxiety when in a group (Gupta, Hariton and Kernberg, 1996).

Informal assessment of the child – in an individual setting

In making an informal assessment it may be useful to observe the characteristics described below, as suggested by Geldard and Geldard (1997):

General appearance: This includes the child's general presentation, how the child is dressed, whether the child is neat and tidy or untidy, the child's level of alertness, the child's physical development, and any obvious discrepancies from normal.

Behaviour: In observing behaviour, the following questions might be asked:

- Is the behaviour quiet, careful, noisy, boisterous, aggressive, or destructive?
- Is the child distractable
- Does the child try to engage in dangerous behaviour?
- Is the child affectionate and dependent on the interaction of the counsellor?
- Is the child defensive, responsive or searching for contact?
- Does the child have appropriate boundaries?
- What is the child's response to physical contact?
- Does the child show approach avoidance tendances?

Mood or Affect: Observing the child's mood or affect may give an indication of his or her underlying emotional state. Children may be observed as being happy, sad, angry, depressed, excited, etc. Some will show little or no emotion. Others will be self-absorbed.

Intellectual functioning and thinking processes: For younger children, observation of intellectual functioning and thinking processes can be carried out by inviting the child to engage in specific tasks such as doing puzzles, naming body parts and identifying colours. For older children general conversation may give an indication of his or her ability to solve problems and conceptualise. It may also give an indication of the child's level of insight, and of the child's understanding of the reason for the assessment session.

Checking the child's sense of reality and organisation of thoughts may unearth abnormal thought patterns if these are present. This check can be done by asking the child who and where he or she is, what day it is, what time it is and by asking about recent events.

Speech and language: Initial assessment of speech and language skills can be made by engaging the child in conversation. Whether the child tends to rely on non-verbal or verbal methods of communication can be observed.

Motor skills: Gross and fine motor coordination can be observed by asking the child to take part in suitable activities and noting whether the child walks, jumps, runs, squats and moves in and out of position with ease or with difficulty. Whether the child appears to be constricted or free in physical expression can also be observed.

Play: Observing a child's play behaviour can give an indication of his or her level of development. It is helpful to observe whether the child is appropriately creative or stereotypic, repetitive or limited.

Child's relationship with the leader: The child's relationship with the leader may be indicated by his or her warmth, friendliness, eye contact, social skill level and predominant interactional style. Whether a child is withdrawn, isolated, friendly, trusting, mistrustful, negativistic or cooperative can be observed.

Child's self-perception: The child's self-perception can be explored by asking questions about his or her understanding and feelings about him/herself, the assessment process, feelings about school and feelings towards friends and family.

As well as observing the child, it may be desirable to ask questions related to some of the assumptions the leader has made about the target group. For example, when interviewing a child for possible inclusion in a group for children who have witnessed violence in the home, it may be relevant to ask questions which relate to the child's perceptions concerning family relationships, parental relationships, problem solving strategies within the family, violence and safety issues.

Informal assessment of the child – in a group setting

There are a number of limitations when assessing a child on his or her own. The context of the interview will be unfamiliar for the child, who will be in the presence of a stranger (the group leader) and may be anxious about the leader's expectations. This is likely to influence the child's behaviour. Additionally, the setting has limitations as there will be no opportunity for the leader to observe social relationship behaviours with peers.

In a group setting the ability to relate with peers may be assessed, but there are also some limitations. Children joining a strange group set up for assessment purposes may behave in atypical ways as a consequence of the stress of peer interactions with unfamiliar children. For example, children may become unusually withdrawn, regressed or aggressive in order to cope with the stress of being in an unfamiliar group setting.

A group setting provides the leader with different information from that obtained in individual assessment. Information obtained from both individual and group assessment is the most useful in helping leaders to select children who will benefit from a group and contribute to the group process.

When observing children in a group setting it may be helpful to use guidelines developed by Gupta, Hariton and Kernberg (1996) in their observations of children in diagnostic groups. Their guidelines were devised for assessment situations where children were permitted to play freely with limited structure in a playroom setting, in the presence of a group leader. In summary, these guidelines suggest that leaders observe the following:

The child's ability to separate from the parent or carer: Leaders may notice whether the child separates easily, or after some reassurance or is reluctant to enter the room.

The way a child relates with the play material: Some children may use materials in an age appropriate way and in the way it is intended to be used. Other children may be destructive, wilfully or unintentionally.

The child's interactions with other children: The way the child relates to other children can be observed by noticing whether the child approaches others easily, whether the child initiates and maintains contact with individual children only and resists group interactions or whether the child has fleeting unsustained contact with others.

The quality of the child's interactions: How the child interacts with other children can be observed by noticing predominantly positive contact such as sharing and turn taking, or predominantly negative contact such as shouting, crying and verbal and physical aggression.

Conflict resolution skills: The way in which the child resolves conflict may be observed. This may vary from being collaborative, retreating from conflict interactions, threatening or manipulative behaviour, or terminating social exchanges.

How the child relates to the leader in the group setting: The child may ignore or avoid the leader, gravitate and become clingy, respond positively or become defiant and oppositional.

The impact of the child on the group: It can be useful to observe whether the child takes on the role of leader or follower, is disruptive of group activities or shows initiative in creating or joining with new themes.

The impact of the group on the child: Observations may be made as to whether the child adapts readily to rules or norms, conforms with the whole group's changes in behaviour, becomes overt or covert in defying the group or detaches from the group.

Formal assessment

There are two important reasons for considering the use of formal assessments. These are:

1. To determine a child's needs and suitability for group work, leaders may wish to use formal assessment instruments in addition to using clinical observation.
2. To enable leaders to measure change in individual children on specific dimensions over the life of a group. This can be useful in evaluating the usefulness of a group programme.

There are a number of psychometric and functional assessment instruments available for assessment of specific characteristics of children. A selection of these is listed in Table 6.1.

Table 6.1   Assessment instruments for use with children

Title	Author/s	Description
Adaptive Behaviour Inventory for Children	Mercer and Lewis (1982)	Measures the child's social role performance in the family, peer group and community by means of an interview with the parent or guardian.
Adaptive Behavior Assessment System	Harrison and Oakland (2000)	Gives a complete assessment of adaptive behaviour functioning.
Adolescent Coping Scale	Frydenberg and Lewis (1993)	Assesses adaptive coping strategies focusing on what young people do rather than what they feel they should be doing.
Behaviour Assessment System for Children	Reynolds and Kamphaus (1992)	Evaluates the behaviours thoughts and emotions of children and adolescents in respect of both personality and behaviour. Adaptive as well as problematic behaviours are measured.
Brown Attention Deficit Disorder Scales – Children's Version	Brown (2000)	Used for ADD diagnosis and treatment monitoring. Focuses on cognitive and affective aspects of ADD.
Carey Temperament Scales	Carey (1995)	Provides measurement of a child's temperament or behavioural style.
Child Behaviour Checklist	Achenbach and Edelbrock (1991)	Designed to obtain standardised data on children's competencies and problems as reported by their parents.
Children's Depression Inventory	Kovacs (1992)	Measures depression in children and adolescents. Ideal for quick screening.
Comprehensive Behaviour Rating Scale for Children	Neeper, Lahey, and Frick (1990)	Provides information about cognitive, emotional and behavioural function that will assist in the development of treatment programmes.
Conners' Rating Scales – Revised	Conners (1997)	Includes measures of Attention Deficit Hyperactivity Disorder in children and adolescents.
Coopersmith Self Esteem Inventories	Coopersmith (1981)	A brief self-report questionnaire measuring attitudes towards the self in social academic and personal contacts.
Devereux Behaviour Rating Scale – School Form	Naglieri, LeBuffe, and Pfeiffer (1993)	Evaluates the existence of behaviours which indicate severe emotional disturbance. Provides information for treatment planning and for evaluating treatment effectiveness.

Table 6.1   (cont'd)

Group Environment Scale	Moos and Humphrey (1986)	Measures group processes in terms of 10 scores: cohesion, leader support, expressiveness, independence, task orientation, self-discovery, anger and aggression, order and organisation, leader control and innovation.
Piers Harris Children's Self Concept Scale	Piers and Harris (1984)	Provides information on the psychological health of children based on the child's own perceptions rather than on parent or teacher information.
Revised Children's Manifest Anxiety Scale	Reynolds and Richmond (1985)	A personality assessment providing measures of anxiety also provides a means of identifying problems and opening avenues for discussion with troubled children.
Sentence Completion Test	Rohde Jansen (1957)	A projective technique suitable for group or individual use. Responses are interpreted in terms of behaviour reactions or forces emanating from the child and from the environment.
Social Skills Rating System	Gresham and Elliott (1990)	A group of norm referenced behaviour rating scales designed to identify social competence and adaptive behaviour in children.

Generally, formal assessments demand a particular level of competence in administration, scoring and interpretation. Leaders must recognise the limits of their competence and use only those assessments for which they are adequately trained. It should be noted that many of the listed assessment instruments are restricted for use by professionals with specific training in their use. Readers should refer to suppliers' catalogues for full details of assessments available and restrictions regarding their use.

Formal assessment of individual children may be helpful in suggesting which children might be usefully put together in a group so that common needs can be addressed. For example, all children scoring poorly in a particular sub-section of the Piers–Harris Children's Self-Concept Scale (Piers and Harris, 1984) might be grouped together on the assumption that they have similar needs.

An advantage of using formal assessments is that results are likely to be less susceptible to subjective error. Formal assessment instruments are standardised and reliable. They are also normed so that results for children being assessed can be compared with norms for the same age and gender. Before carrying out formal assessments, their use and the reasons for their use need to be discussed with the children concerned and their parent/s or carer/s. Informed parental/carer permission to carry out the selected assessment procedure can then be obtained. Where formal assessment is used, the parent/s or carer/s have a right to be given the results with accompanying interpretation.

It is important for leaders to recognise the influence of socioeconomic, ethnic and cultural factors on assessment scores and to allow for these factors when making decisions about whether to include or exclude a child from a group.

Selection of a particular assessment instrument needs to be based on its usefulness in measuring variables relevant to inclusion or exclusion of a child in a group, and/or variables relevant to the goals of a group programme.

Assessing parents and families

When deciding whether or not to include a child in a group programme it can be very useful to ascertain the parent/s' or carer/s' attitudes to the programme. Additionally, in some cases, it may be useful to meet with the family. This is because lack of parental and family support for participation in a programme may militate against the achievement of useful gains for the child, whereas parental and family support may help produce the desired outcomes (Tuckman, 1995; Waas and Graczyk, 1998).

For some children the involvement of their school may be desirable. For example, in a study evaluating the treatment of depressed children, evidence suggested the need for an integration of different variables with the involvement of family, parents and school (Stark *et al.*, 1991).

When talking with the parents or carers and family it can be useful to explore the following:

- The parents' or carer/s' impressions of relationships within the family
- The parents' or carer/s' principle concerns regarding their child's behaviour
- Parenting issues and expectations, parenting style and disciplinary methods
- Hopes and expectations regarding outcomes if the child is involved in the group programme

- Whether the parent/s' or carer/s' are willing and able to attend an information session, if required
- Whether transport can be arranged to bring the child to and from group sessions on a regular basis for the duration of the group

For certain types of group it may be important to check out information directly related to the needs of the target group. For example, when running groups for children who have been exposed to domestic violence, it is desirable to check out the following:

- Does the child currently have contact with the perpetrator of the violence?
- Has the child received any injuries as a result of becoming involved in the domestic violence?
- Is there evidence of internalised problems in the child (for example, fear, depression, withdrawal, poor body image, low self esteem, lethargy or feelings of shame)?
- Is there evidence of externalised behaviours resulting from the child's experience (for example, aggression, temper tantrums, destructive behaviour, lying, or delinquency)?

Another important issue relates to confidentiality. For groups to be therapeutically effective, the children need to feel free to talk about any of the issues troubling them. They will not feel free to do this if they believe there might be negative consequences. For this reason issues of confidentiality and the possible disclosure of private family information need to be explored with parent/s or carer/s during the assessment phase. Similarly, when groups are run in schools, such issues may need to be discussed with teachers in order to enable the children to feel free to disclose information that is troubling for them.

Interviews with parent/s or carer/s and their children can be useful in determining medical, dietary and other specific needs, as well as for finding out who will collect the child after each session.

Parental involvement

Whenever the parents' or carers' interest warrants it, a meeting for them prior to the first children's group session needs to be organised to let them know what they can expect to occur in the children's group. Having a meeting with parents or carers to orient them to the programme and to answer their questions is very useful in gaining their cooperation. This is valuable because parent/s or carer/s who encourage their children to attend and participate and who cooperate and collaborate with leaders promote the success of the group and the child's well-being (Rose, S.R., 1998; Rose and Edleson, 1987).

Sometimes it may be useful to run a parents' or carers' group in parallel with a children's group. This can certainly be useful, but is costly as staff are needed to run this extra group. Parallel groups for parents or carers can be useful in enabling them to accept and facilitate change in their children's behaviour and to assist their children with homework tasks. The children's group facilitators may also gain valuable information from parents which will enable them to address the children's needs more fully.

Parents and carers need to be aware of the goals and purposes of a group so that they can give informed consent for their child to participate and enable them to be supportive of the group work. At times, they may be included in the children's group activities in order to meet particular needs of their children.

In some cases, offering non-custodial parents information about a group is important. Children who have contact with a non-custodial parent may feel uncomfortable if they believe they are betraying that parent by disclosing information about that parent in the group. Also, where a non-custodial parent is not supportive of a child's participation in a group, the child may experience tension in his or her relationship with that parent.

In school settings it is sometimes beneficial for leaders to invite teachers to join specific sessions with the group's consent. This demystifies the activities of the group and promotes better understanding by the teachers.

Feedback of assessment outcome

Once a decision is made to include a child in a group, parent/s or carer/s need to be informed of the decision and given any additional information they need. For example, they need to be reminded of the location and times for the first group session and given information about anything the child needs to bring to the group. It is always wise to ask parents or guardians to sign a consent form agreeing to the participation of their child in any group. Such a consent form needs to be specific to the relevant group and needs to cover issues such as legal, professional and personal liability. If video taping is to be part of group activity, consent forms for this purpose will also be required.

Where a formal assessment has been conducted an interview with the parent/s or carer/s will need to be arranged so that results and interpretation of the assessment can be shared.

Exclusion from the group

When leaders decide not to include a child in a group, it is desirable to try to help the child and parent/s or carer/s to avoid viewing this as rejection. It can often be helpful if a decision to exclude a child is explained by informing the parent/s or carer/s that inclusion would not be in the best interests of the child, and identifying the reasons why this is so. Informal and formal assessment results may be relevant when explaining to parent/s or carer/s the leaders' decision not to include a child in a group. Other alternative treatment options which might address the child's needs should be explored.

Children and parents or carers should be informed that exclusion from one group does not necessarily mean exclusion from all groups. As discussed previously, it may be that exclusion from one group identifies a need for the development of a different group which would be suitable for addressing the child's needs.

7 The leader's role

Leaders of children's groups have to do several things simultaneously while a group is running and this can be demanding. While facilitating the programme, they have to observe, notice and respond to issues concerning the group as a whole, and also attend to the individual needs of group members. Before a group programme begins, leaders need to plan and prepare to meet the practical requirements of the programme. In preparing for and delivering a group programme leaders need to carefully consider the following:

1. Their leadership style.
2. The stages of group development.
3. The needs of individual children.
4. The need for debriefing and supervision.
5. Review and evaluation of the programme.

LEADERSHIP STYLE

Group work with children can be very demanding for leaders, and this is especially so if they are not clear about the style of leadership they wish to use. The style of leadership selected must be consistent with the theoretical approach used, appropriate for the target group and suit the personalities of the leaders.

The theoretical approach to be used will in many cases have a major influence on the style of leadership used. For example, when running a group along cognitive behavioural lines the style of leadership will tend to be didactic and directive, whereas when running a psychoanalytic group the leader will be inclined to be more disengaged and separate from the group, focusing on the interpretation of observations.

Leadership style needs to be suitable for use with the particular target group concerned. For example, when running a group for children with Attention Deficit Hyperactivity Disorder leaders need to contain behaviours and may need to be predominantly authoritarian, whereas when running a group for anxious children a gentler approach might be more suitable.

Leaders also need to take account of their own personality and personality traits so that the style of leadership they use is authentic and genuinely matches their individual personalities. For example, it may be comfortable for a quiet introverted leader to rely on a democratic style of leadership rather than try to be authoritarian. Every leader will have his or her own strengths and limitations. Often leaders have unrealistic expectations of themselves and expect to be able to perform all the required tasks and demonstrate all the required skills needed to run a particular group. This may be impossible and, if so, the use of a co-leader is sensible.

There are many different styles of leadership including:

● Authoritarian
● Democratic
● Laissez-faire
● Pro-active

Authoritarian leadership

Choosing an authoritarian leadership style may mean that all activities of the group are decided by the leader and communicated to the group by the leader. Authoritarian leaders tend to remain aloof from the group and to make personal remarks which are directed either at the whole group or at individual children. These personal remarks may often be controlling so that the group can be managed with safety.

Group participants led by authoritarian leaders tend to react more aggressively and with more dependence upon the leader than those members exposed to other leadership styles (George and Dustan, 1988).

The authoritarian style has the advantages that a safe environment can be created in a group of impulsive and/or destructive children, individual children in the group may feel safe because there is an external locus of control, and tasks can be completed. Disadvantages are that the authoritarian style does not allow for the growth of group cohesion with members becoming interdependent. However, a form of group cohesion may occur with each member becoming dependent on the leader.

Authoritarian leaders use their power to influence children in the group. This influence may have an effect even on those children who try to resist. However, it needs to be recognised that the effect may not always be the one desired by the leaders.

Democratic leadership

When using a democratic leadership style, most rules and decisions are made by the children in the group. Democratic leaders try to seek group consensus so that the decisions of the group reflect the views of individual members. The democratic style requires a leader to help the group achieve goals, but to do this in ways which the group collectively chooses. Thus democratic leaders tend to make objective remarks rather than personal remarks.

The research literature demonstrates that a democratic leadership style has consistently been associated with increased member satisfaction and group cohesion (Wheelan, 1994). Additionally, children in a democratically run group tend to be more productive as they feel included in group decision making. Disadvantages of this style are that it may be impossible to obtain consensus in a group, so at times a leader who wishes to be democratic may need to satisfy only the majority of the group, leaving a minority feeling dissatisfied. This is likely to affect group cohesion with the group tending to be polarised into coalitions and sub-groups. The task, then, for the democratic leader is to help the sub-groups become effective and productive.

Laissez-faire leadership

A laissez-fair leadership style requires minimal participation from the leader. The leader simply supplies materials and only gives information when group members ask for it. This style of leadership encourages the children to adopt various roles within the group, such as leader, helper, supervisor, observer, worker, peacemaker, scapegoat or distracter. This may enable the leaders to observe behaviours which can be usefully processed in order to commend appropriate behaviour and/or facilitate change. Where the assumed roles of individual members are accepted by the whole group there is likely to be a high level of group productivity with positive outcomes. However, where individual children are not competent at fulfilling assumed roles, tension will be generated and there will be lower satisfaction among group members.

Generally, children in groups led by leaders with a laissez-fair style tend to be less satisfied and less organised than participants in groups led by leaders with a democratic style. A laissez-faire group leadership style is not recommended for children with low ego strength. Unfortunately, due to the lack of structure in laissez-faire groups, such children are at risk of being the subject of abuse and maltreatment by other group members.

The pro-active approach to leadership

When running groups for children the authoritarian, democratic or laissez-faire leadership styles can be used. However, whatever style is used the leader does need to be ready to take action to ensure the emotional and physical safety of group members and to maximise the potential for achieving change.

A preferred alternative to using one of the previously discussed styles is to use a pro-active approach which involves using a combination of styles. In the pro-active approach the leader is flexible, so that spontaneous movement from an emphasis on one style to another occurs. Thus, during a group session and over the life of a group leaders vary their style to maximise opportunities occurring in the group, and also to suit the mood and activity of the group at any particular time. The pro-active leadership approach can also be sensitive to the stages of group development, as will be discussed later.

The pro-active approach for working with children in groups is not the same as, but is derived from, the pro-active approach for the individual counselling of adolescents as described by Geldard and Geldard (1999). It requires spontaneous and creative responses to the needs of the group and individual members. It recognises windows of opportunity where counselling strategies can be used to promote the well-being of individual members and the whole group.

Usually the pro-active approach to leadership will make use of a democratic leadership style as the predominant style to allow individuals in the group to feel free to make choices within limits set by the group, while at the same time providing safety. However, being pro-active allows leaders to be authoritarian when appropriate in order to ensure compliance with group rules and to ensure that goals are met. At other times leaders may deliberately use a laissez-faire style for a while to allow children in the group more freedom. During this period of freedom, they can observe the group's interactions, behaviours and social skills. These interactions, behaviours and social skills can then be discussed or 'processed', as described in Chapter 8.

Characteristics of successful leaders

Irrespective of the style of leadership chosen there are certain charac-teristics associated with successful leadership. It is advantageous if leaders:

- Are creative and flexible, genuinely like children, have a sense of humour, are able to tolerate frustration, have a positive outlook on life, are self-confident, open and willing to self-evaluate
- Are able to help each group member feel that he or she is an important member of the group and at the same time be aware of group developmental stages and have the ability to respond appropriately to these stages
- Are professionally knowledgeable in their chosen theoretical approach and are able to use appropriate counselling micro-skills so that they can facilitate and promote change
- Have the stamina and ability to cope with verbal attacks without becoming defensive
- Have insight into their own issues, particularly those issues relating to control, power, dependence and independence

Co-leadership

It is often preferable to have two leaders working together. Two leaders offer two sets of observations, two perspectives and a broader expertise. They may complement each other's strengths and weak-nesses and their relationship can serve as a successful role model for relationships for the children (Siepker and Kandaras, 1985). Addition-ally, there are advantages for inexperienced leaders in working with a more experienced leader. Joint work may provide professional and personal growth and learning.

Having two leaders is especially sensible for those groups where there is a high degree of disturbance in a group. It is a practical necessity for groups where there is the possibility of violent behaviour. For children's groups in general there are considerable advantages in having two leaders, as one can attend to the whole group while the other attends to individuals with specific needs. Additionally, if there is only one leader, a child is more likely to drop out if tension arises between that child and the leader. In contrast, if there are two leaders, then that child may join with the co-leader whose active and supportive role may enable the child to stay in the group during times of high anxiety, instead of dropping out.

When there are two leaders, it is essential for them to have a good working relationship with each other. Any negative feelings that arise either before, during or after the group need to be talked through. If satisfactory resolution does not occur, then them need to seek joint supervision from a counsellor. If resolution of the leaders' differences cannot be achieved, the children in the group may parallel the maladaptive relationship behaviours of the leaders with disastrous consequences.

Leaders and sweepers

Before the start of a group session, it is essential that leaders agree about their individual roles and responsibilities. A preferred model is for one leader to take the role of *leader* and the other to take the role of *sweeper*. Each time the group meets the leaders can, if they wish, reverse roles, so that the group does not associate leadership with one person. This is particularly important when the co-leaders are of opposite gender.

The *leader's* role involves directly organising and processing group activities as discussed in Chapter 8. It is the leader who makes decisions about what to do next, and is generally seen to be in charge.

The *sweeper's* role is different, but equally important. The sweeper has the following duties:

- To be supportive of the leader
- To attend to individual problems within the group when these cannot be dealt with in a whole group setting
- To fetch and carry materials
- To attend to issues that may arise as a result of a group process

An example of an issue which might be dealt with by a sweeper is dealing with the difficult behaviour of one individual if dealing with this in the whole group setting might be counter-productive for the child concerned, or might seriously intrude on an important group process.

THE STAGES OF GROUP DEVELOPMENT

All groups change and develop over time as group members develop group norms, values and ideas (Shaw, 1981) and are influenced by the group context (Lewin, Lippitt and White, 1994). From the time when group members first meet to the time when a group disbands, a developmental process occurs (Posthuma, 1996). This developmental process has been described by many authors including George and Dustin (1988), Kymissis (1996), Siepker and Kandaras (1985), Tuckman and Jensen (1977), Watson *et al.* (1981), and Wheelan (1994). Although there are differences between the descriptions of various authors, there is also considerable similarity.

Watson *et al.* (1981), in a synthesis of the work of Tuckman (1995), described group development as having five stages. These five stages are commonly referred to as the 'forming', 'storming', 'norming', 'performing' and 'mourning' stages. George and Dustin (1988) refer to only four stages of group development. Although these stages have different titles to those of Watson *et al.* (1981), they are broadly similar, but with the norming and performing stages combined into a single stage. Fatout (1996), describes four stages of group development in children's groups. These four stages have some differences in emphasis, but are somewhat similar in content to the four stages described by George and Dustin (1988).

Siepker and Kandaras (1985) describe six group stages for therapy groups for children as they include a preparatory stage which occurs before the group starts and a closure stage which occurs after the group ends.

In the author's experience, a four stage model which covers the actual group experience, with the addition of preparation and closure stages, generally describes the developmental stages of groups for children. Hence the following stages will be discussed:

Stage 1: Preparation
Stage 2: Forming
Stage 3: Storming
Stage 4: Norming
Stage 5: Mourning
Stage 6: Closure

Stages two to five do not occur discretely. They may overlap and there may be some regression at times to a previous stage. A whole group may not move through the stages at the same pace, as some individual children or sub-groups may progress more slowly than others.

Stage one: the preparation stage

This stage begins from the time that the initial idea that it might be useful to run a group is floated. In the preparation stage there is often considerable ambivalence by staff in any agency considering running a group for children. Some staff may be excited by the prospect, but others may be anxious. They may be concerned about the impact of the group on the normal staff workload and worried about the intrusion of the group into part of their working space.

Agencies need to take time to attend to the practical, physical and psychological requirements associated with running a group. Everyone needs to be prepared for the initial screening interviews, otherwise staff may become stressed and parents and children involved may be affected by this.

The preparation stage includes the intake and assessment procedures described in Chapter 6. During this stage a relationship begins between individual children and the leaders. This relationship is important as it will colour the children's attitudes and motivations with regard to joining the group.

Stage two: the forming stage

The forming stage starts at the beginning of the first group session. It is a time of orientation and exploration. It is normal for both children and leaders to feel anxious at the start of the first group. This anxiety is useful as it provides the energy required for success. After being together for a while, with supportive facilitation, most children will discover that their fears are unjustified. Relief from the initial anxiety tends to raise the spirit and morale in the group (Lampel, 1985).

During the forming stage group members develop a sense of trust, safety and belonging. Often a group leader can help to create trust by modelling behaviour which illustrates that he or she is prepared to trust the group. For example, appropriate self-disclosure by a leader can often encourage children in a group to feel safe in self-disclosing themselves.

Dependency is an important issue during the forming stage. Because the group is not well established most children will tend to be dependent on direct guidance from the leaders rather than taking risks in promoting their own ideas. It can be useful to remind children of the reasons why they have been included in the group and to let them know what they are going to do in the group.

During the forming stage the leaders need to continue to observe and assess each child so that they can respond appropriately to perceived individual needs while at the same time ensuring that individual behaviours are not damaging the joining process.

At this early stage of group development it is prudent for leaders to give feedback to other workers in their agency regarding the development of the group. They may also wish to ask others for feedback regarding the impact of the group on individuals and the agency generally. By doing this, other workers may be encouraged to view the group positively.

An indication that the forming stage has been successful is when the children have invested enough in the group to personalise and label it as 'my group' (Lampel, 1985). When this occurs they have developed a sense of belonging.

Stage three: the storming stage

Invitations made in the 'forming' stage to share, express feelings and accept others will hopefully create a climate of safety and trust in which group members feel able to express themselves with little fear of criticism or reprimand. If this is achieved, the environment will be one which is suitable for producing change.

The occurrence of change is often characterised by conflict, dominance, resistance, inclusion, confrontation and rebellion, which is why this stage is referred to as the 'storming' stage. During this stage children will test themselves, each other as well as the leaders, and behaviours that are resistant, monopolising, silent or manipulative are likely to be observed. Increased feelings of safety allow dissent to occur. Dissatisfaction with group goals and values emerges. Decreased conformity and increased individual participation replace conformity and dependency on the leaders.

As group members feel freer to criticise each other and/or to assert their own points of view, conflict may develop. Some children may behave in an inconsistent manner, being aggressive at first and then very quiet, while others may be quiet and share only their most acceptable thoughts and feelings with the group.

The 'storming' stage is often a time when sub-groups will develop. This occurs particularly with children aged nine to twelve. Usually the formation of sub-groups is not willingly accepted by the rest of the group, so conflict arises. Individuals in sub-groups, or the whole group, may become shrill and loud, very active or withdrawn and/or rebellious. There may be a sense of movement, sound and feeling constantly moving to a crescendo. As anxiety rises, individual children may seek escape from this through withdrawal, silence, attempting to leave physically or wildly acting out (Lewis, 1985). The child is seeking to explore, test and understand the leaders' boundaries and role.

The effects of transference will be important during the storming stage, with some children challenging leaders whom they perceive as like their parents or teachers. During this stage the children need to test out their beliefs about their leaders so that they feel comfortable in knowing what to expect.

Resistance may be directed towards the content of a group session, towards the whole group or the leaders. This may be expressed through withdrawal, absence from the group, questioning the purpose of the group or attacking others. While this storming phase may be a difficult and unpleasant stage for group leaders, it does present an opportunity for a leader to demonstrate openness to, and non-defensive acceptance of, criticism so that group members can model on this behaviour. By facing the group's attacks and challenges, the leaders have an opportunity to encourage the sharing of thoughts and feelings and to reinforce the appropriateness of such sharing. They will also need to manage the inappropriate acting out behaviour of some children (see Chapter 8).

During the storming stage leaders often experience a sense of failure, believing they are failing to lead the group successfully because the harmonious, constructively working group they envisaged has not been achieved. Although this is a natural response, it would be more appropriate for them to say to themselves, 'we have been so successful in the task of completing the forming stage of group development that the group has naturally and appropriately moved into the storming stage.'

In the storming stage, leaders need to be congruent, open with the children, and aware and concerned for them. They must, however, remain grounded, exuding feelings of strength, patience and positive acceptance.

Stage four: the norming stage

If efforts to resolve conflicts are successful during the storming stage, there will be an increased consensus about group goals and culture, leading to increased trust and cohesion in the group. This marks the beginning of the norming stage. The norming stage is characterised by a quietening of processes as a consequence of more cohesiveness in the group. Group members experience a sense of belonging and there is an increased level of acceptance of each other by members of the group. Anxiety is present but belongs to each child. It is no longer diffuse, free floating or threatening to disrupt the group (Kandaras, 1985).

This stage is marked by productivity and mutuality, with group members working towards understanding each other as they change behaviours, beliefs and attitudes. Often children in this stage will begin to disclose more freely and share personal experiences relevant to group topics, having achieved feelings of safety and a belief that self-disclosure can result in positive rather than negative consequences. It is important for leaders to encourage group members to disclose real-life information during this stage of group development. Such self-disclosure can then be used to help individuals move into taking action to change their behaviours and experience self-improvement.

Some children may begin to worry about not being liked, or not being close to children they would like to be close to. Alternatively they may have anxiety about being too close to others, as this is a stage where group cohesion is at its highest. Additionally, there is an increased tolerance of sub-groups. While conflict may continue to occur, conflict management strategies tend to be more effective than previously. The leaders' role can consequently become less directive and more facilitative.

Although trust is required for effective work to occur, it is advantageous if a balance between comfort and anxiety can be established. It is desirable for the children in a group to feel reasonably comfortable and at ease, but the presence, at times, of a low level of anxiety can be helpful in motivating them. This is especially useful when trying to promote change in attitudes or behaviours. However, it is important to monitor and control anxiety levels because high levels of anxiety are likely to inhibit children from participating spontaneously and interacting freely with others.

Stage five: the mourning stage

Ending a group is often a difficult experience both for group members and for leaders. The children's ability to manage conflict may deteriorate. Commitment to tasks may either increase or decrease abruptly, and the children may avoid problematic issues.

It is wise to give children sufficient warning that their group is going to disband, as they need to be given the opportunity to prepare for the end of their group experience. Two sessions before the last the leaders might give the group a reminder that the programme is nearing its end, and then give another reminder the following week. The children might be invited to make suggestions of activities they would like to include in the last session.

By recognising that the group is moving towards closure, the children have the opportunity to review and gain a clear picture of their overall experience in the group. For some groups, the way in which the children cope with the ending may be dependent on the degree of change or growth that has occurred within them during the group experience. An important goal for this stage is for the children to separate, as successfully as possible, while maintaining and utilizing the gains they have made through participating in the group (Herndon, 1985).

Group leaders need to give participants an opportunity to share their emotional feelings and thoughts related to leaving the group. This may include sharing positive and negative feelings about having participated in the group process as well as sharing feelings of anger, sadness or disappointment because the group is ending. It is important to help group members to put into words what they have learned from the group experience. This can either be done through the use of open discussion, symbolic activities or evaluation sheets designed to help participants focus on and talk about their experiences.

Stage 6: closure

The closure stage starts after the last group session has finished. Although the individual children in the group no longer relate in the group setting, leaders may need to give them and/or their parents or carers feedback regarding their participation in the group and/or information regarding possible future programmes, activities or treatment. Leaders therefore need to carefully consider the ongoing needs, if any, of the children concerned.

In this stage, leaders need to evaluate the programme and their own performance as leaders (see Chapter 9). This process needs to involve debriefing with a supervisor.

Progression through the stages of group development

Progression through the stages of group development will be influenced by whether the group is open or closed, the leadership style and degree of structure in the group, the type of group (for example, psycho-educational, counselling, support or therapeutic) and the theoretical approach used. Progression is not usually linear. Some children in a group may progress faster than others, there may be regression at times to a previous stage, or progress through the stages may be blocked for a while.

Open and closed groups

The effect of open versus closed groups on the group developmental process is quite significant, not in terms of disrupting that process, but in how it is manifested. In closed groups the developmental stages are generally more predictable, in such a way that each group session builds on the previous ones. In open groups where individual children's short term membership changes over time, the developmental stages follow a different but predictable pattern. Each time a new child joins the group, other members are likely to regress to an earlier stage of group development during the integration process. Each time a member leaves the group, the remaining group members will experience a loss (Dies, 1996).

Although in closed groups the developmental stages are more predictable, these groups are still susceptible to the influence of events which might disturb the equilibrium of the group. We have noticed that when such events occur, some members in the group, or the whole group, might regress to an earlier stage of group development.

Leadership style

Wheelan (1994) believes that it may be useful to vary the leadership style used as a group proceeds through the stages of development. She points out that in the second stage, forming, groups are heavily dependent on their leaders to function effectively, hence a directive leadership style may be useful in helping the group to feel safe. In stage three, storming, groups are testing their ability to organise and prepare for successful work. At this stage, leaders who are supportive and participatory but not particularly directive, may be successful in facilitating the group's growth. In the fourth stage, norming, because the group has developed the ability to work together, little input from the leaders is necessary. In fact, more directive leadership may interfere with group processes.

Wheelan's approach is likely to be useful for some target groups and some types of group. Clearly, leaders need to be knowledgeable about the needs of the children in a group, the goals of the group and their theoretical framework when deciding whether or not it would be beneficial to vary their leadership style during a group programme.

THE NEEDS OF INDIVIDUAL CHILDREN

While attending to issues which develop for the whole group as it progresses through the stages of forming, storming, norming and mourning, leaders also need to attend to the issues of individual children.

As discussed in Chapter 6, before joining a group each child should be assessed to determine his or her readiness to deal and cope with the demands of the group. During this assessment process knowledge about each child is gained together with a general understanding of how that child's individual needs meet the criteria for the target group.

To meet the individual needs of each child while in a group, leaders must:

1. Provide opportunities for self-awareness and personal learning.
2. Provide opportunities for vicarious learning.
3. Observe and attend to individual behaviours.

Self-awareness and personal learning

Groups are useful in helping raise children's awareness of their behaviours because they provide an opportunity for self-disclosure and the receipt of feedback from others. Both self-disclosure and the receipt of feedback during group processes have been identified as being useful for increasing personal learning (Bloch, 1986) and for providing opportunities and options for change.

As a group develops, individuals within it begin to interact with one another in a similar way to the way they interact with others in their lives. The group becomes a 'laboratory' where a variety of behaviours can be exhibited. As members receive feedback from others, they learn about the effects of their behaviours on others. Feedback, which is given with care and support, enables them to understand the impact their behaviours have on others, and to learn how their behaviours create specific reactions from others. As a result, they may make decisions which result in changed behaviours.

As individual children in a group become more aware of the impact of their behaviours on the feelings of others, and more aware of the opinions that others have of them, they start to recognise their own responsibility for what occurs as a result of their communication with other children. In order to help children to benefit from this kind of self-awareness and interpersonal learning, it can be helpful if group leaders focus on current 'here and now' interactional behaviours in the group.

Group leaders need to use counselling skills appropriate for their theoretical approach. For example, leaders using an experiential therapies approach will use counselling skills intended to heighten the children's awareness of their current emotional and cognitive experiences. Leaders may also wish to make use of group processes to reflect, explain and interpret behaviours and responses which have been observed.

Often, open and accurate self-disclosure by a group leader can provide useful information relevant to group processes. For example, if a group leader feels impatient, discouraged, bored or frustrated, then sharing this information with the group may result in discussion that will help the group discover underlying processes and may enable group members to make useful and adaptive changes.

Vicarious learning

Vicarious learning has been called 'spectator therapy' (George and Dustin, 1988). The words 'spectator therapy' imply that the individual needs of children in a group can sometimes be met by their observation of other members. Sometimes group leaders can help children learn vicariously by discussing group processes which involve other group members who have similar issues. In doing this, the children may gain insight into what is occurring within themselves and may recognise things which apply to others and fit for themselves as well as things which apply to others and do not fit for themselves. Hence, identification with other members in a group can be used as part of a group process to facilitate learning about self.

Observing and attending to individual behaviours

Some individual children may have unexpected and excessive responses to a group programme. For example, they may demonstrate high levels of anxiety, become dissociative, regress, and/or withdraw as a consequence of the programme content and/or the responses of other children. For some of these children it may be possible to attend to their needs in a whole group setting by using appropriate intervention strategies and counselling skills. For other children this may not be possible. In this case, while one leader continues to address the needs of the group, a co-leader may need to attend to the child in question by exploring that child's personal feelings and issues triggered by the group programme. As a consequence of such an intervention the child may be able to re-adjust to the group programme, or, if not, the child's membership of the group may need to be re-addressed.

THE INFLUENCE OF GROUP STRUCTURE

To some extent the type of structure used must depend on the type of group and the theoretical approach of the leaders. For example, in psycho-educational groups where the emphasis is on learning, education and prevention, a relatively high degree of structure may be required. Such groups are usually set up to address particular themes such as AIDS prevention, substance abuse and suicide prevention (Jaffe and Kalman, 1991). In counselling and psychotherapy groups the degree of structure required is likely to be less, in order to allow the group to move more freely in the direction that it needs. Clearly, the degree of structure will significantly affect group processes.

In groups that rely on minimal structure, the processes which emerge naturally in the group may be very conducive to personal growth. In such groups there may be more opportunity for children to develop empathic and supportive relationships with each other. Minimal structure may also encourage risk-taking in sharing information. When levels of structure are low, it can be helpful if leaders draw the group's attention to, and discuss, changes in its interactions over time. Doing this may promote change.

Groups where there is a relatively high level of structure tend to be task oriented. This requires commitment from individual members to stay on a task as well as to offer support and social reinforcement to other children in the group. In such structured groups, the group processes will be directly influenced by the group leaders.

The structure leaders choose will depend not only on the type of group and theoretical approach, but will also be influenced by the leaders' personality, ability to use humour, awareness of processes occurring and the goals for the group. The structure of a group will also be influenced by the strategies used to manage unacceptable behaviours (see Chapter 8).

DEBRIEFING AND SUPERVISION

Successful group leadership demands that leaders and co-leaders debrief after each session. Debriefing is useful to enable leaders to:

- Deal with their own issues in their relationship with each other
- Deal with their own issues which may have interfered with the group process
- Provide feedback and support for each other
- Provide an opportunity for expression of discomfort or pleasure about the group session generally
- Evaluate what was successful and what could have been done differently
- Discuss changes which may be needed next time the group meets
- Discuss emerging needs of individual children

To ensure accountability, review and evaluation of every group programme is essential. As part of the overall evaluation, an evaluation procedure should be used at the end of each group session (see Chapter 9). Additionally, it is essential that group leaders have access to professional supervision by a qualified counsellor.

Supervision

There is a strong need for leaders to undergo training and supervision if their work is to be maximally effective. It is highly desirable for new leaders to have the opportunity to work with or observe experienced leaders before running a group themselves. Also, it is desirable for leaders to have experience of being a group member themselves so that they have personal experience of what it is like to be in a group. Additionally, leaders of counselling and therapy groups do need to have undergone personal psychotherapeutic or self-exploratory work.

Group leaders need to be aware that transference and counter-transference issues can dominate leader–child relationships in a group. Children may perceive a leader as similar to a parent and respond accordingly. They may become dependent on an idealised parental figure. A leader may then, in response, inadvertently take up the parent role and fall into wanting to rescue, protect and nurture. The need to have a level of control and to set boundaries can easily trigger counter-transference responses in a leader. This in turn may result in acting out behaviour in the child (Dwivedi, 1993b).

In order to deal with issues of transference and counter-transference effectively, leaders need to be continually monitoring their own feelings and behaviours. Leaders need to be able to handle a deluge of various unconscious manifestations of hostility from children in a group. When this happens, they will be confronted by material that inevitably recalls their own, perhaps troubled, childhood experiences (Kraft, 1996). Identified problems then need to be addressed either during debriefing and/or supervision.

A variety of supervisory methods are effective: dyadic, for example, involving a leader and supervisor, or triadic, involving leader, co-leader and supervisor. When triadic supervision is used, focus can be on the development of the co-therapy relationship and it effects on the group, as well as the assessment of the group and its members (Siepker and Kandaras, 1985). However, where individual issues are too personal to resolve in a triad, individual supervision is required.

Sometimes supervision may take place in a group setting. This is particularly useful where a number of leaders are running groups simultaneously. Participation in group supervision has the advantage that leaders experience being group members themselves during supervision. In this way, they can experience first-hand processes such as resistance and cohesion, and other group phenomena which will occur in the groups they are running during the stages of group development.

Supervision may be enhanced through the use of video-taping and observation by supervisors through one-way mirrors.

8 Counselling and facilitation skills required in children's groups

A primary role of group leaders is that of facilitator. Facilitation involves running the planned programme and during group sessions observing and influencing group processes so that goals for individual children and the group can be met. Group processes involve the interactions that occur between individual group members on a one-to-one basis and between individual group members and the group as a whole. The leaders themselves are included in these processes. Group processes therefore include individual and group communication, behaviours, relationships and attitudes. These will be influenced by the degree of structure, leadership style and type of group.

The type of activities used will also influence group processes. Therefore activities need to be purposefully selected to encourage the group to interact in ways that promote the achievement of goals. While the children are involved in activities the leaders need to observe and tune into the interactions occurring between the children. Staying in touch with the moment-to-moment process enables leaders to make best use of the programme in order to meet the needs of the children. It also enables them to recognise critical incidents.

A critical incident is any process which, when it occurs in the group, provides an opportunity for a leader to respond in order to promote change (Cohen and Smith, 1976). The change to be promoted may involve an individual child, the whole group or relationships within the group. An effective leader will be vigilant and quick to recognise critical incidents as they occur so that, if appropriate, the opportunity to intervene with the goal of producing change can be seized. Leaders do not need to respond to every critical incident as to do so might adversely affect the flow and continuity of the programme. Instead, a leader may sometimes decide that it is in the best interests of the group and/or individual children to ignore a critical incident. This is particularly relevant in the early stages of group formation where leaders may wish to observe patterns of behaviour before intervening.

To make best use of a programme and respond to critical incidents leaders need to make use of counselling skills, processing skills, facilitation skills and behaviour management skills.

COUNSELLING SKILLS

The counselling skills used will depend on the type of group and the theoretical approach of the leaders. The skills discussed below are most suitable for topic-focused groups where leaders choose an integrated theoretical approach and a pro-active leadership style (see Chapter 7). Counselling micro-skills, for use in children's groups, can broadly be grouped under the following headings:

- Observation
- Active listening
- Giving feedback
- Use of questions
- Confronting
- Disclosure skills

Observation

Observation skills have been described in Chapter 6. When using these skills leaders may usefully observe not only current behaviours and social skills, but also changes in these over the life of the group. The programme may then be adjusted, if necessary, to meet changes in perceived needs.

Active listening

Active listening skills are particularly useful when encouraging children to share personal information with a group and to facilitate self-disclosure. Active listening skills include non-verbal responses, encouragers, reflection of content and feelings, summarising, and accenting and amplifying.

Non-verbal responses include nods of the head, changes in facial expression and changes in body posture. They give messages without the use of words.

Encouragers are minimal verbal responses which let a child know that what he or she is saying is being heard and implicitly invite the child to continue. They include expressions such as, 'Mm', 'Uh-ha', 'Yes', 'Really' and 'Right'.

Reflection of content helps the child to feel heard and validated. When reflecting content, a leader paraphrases in his or her own words what the child has said. For example, a leader might say, 'You prefer to have the light on at night because it makes you feel safer', if a child has been talking about his or her fears about going to sleep, or, 'You'd like to be able to do what your brothers and sisters do', if a child has been talking about perceived unfairness in the family.

Reflection of feelings is likely to encourage a child to get in touch with the reflected feeling. A leader might reflect feelings of sadness, anxiety, or excitement by using the following expressions: 'You're sad' or 'You are feeling sad', 'You are worried' or 'You are feeling worried', 'You're excited' or 'You're feeling excited'.

Often reflection of content and feelings can be combined. For example a leader might say: 'You get frightened when your parents argue with each other', after a child has disclosed that he or she hides when his/her dad and mum shout at each other.

Summarising enables a leader to feed back to the group a concise synopsis of what has been discussed so that the children are able to grasp the central themes of the discussion.

Giving feedback

Giving feedback helps individual members and the group become aware of the behaviours that are occurring in the group. Feedback may be given to the group as a whole by using a comment such as 'I notice that there is a lot of interrupting in the group', or by saying to an individual 'Billy, you are very active'.

Sometimes feedback will be given with the intention of drawing attention to a group process which may be affecting two or more people. For example, a leader might say 'Mary, I notice that whenever Fred says anything, you give a big sigh'. This might allow Mary to talk about her feelings towards Fred, might encourage Fred to look at his behaviour or might give other members of the group the opportunity to comment on their perceptions and feelings related to the group process.

Giving feedback can be valuable to members of the group who are not mentioned in the feedback, as they may learn vicariously from the feedback and subsequent discussion.

Feedback can be used to give affirmation and for normalising, reframing and cheer-leading. It can also be useful to encourage, shape and guide behaviours. For example, in order to allow a child to pass and miss a turn in a game but still feel good, a leader might say 'You need time to think about that'.

Rose and Edleson (1987) provide sensible guidelines for giving feedback to children who have been rehearsing new behaviours by role-playing. They suggest giving positive feedback first, so that the child receives reinforcement for engaging in the role-play and is then more open to receiving criticism. Feedback needs to be specific and criticism should be couched in terms of actions or statements that could have been used as alternatives to those that were used. For example, a leader might begin by saying 'Mary, you did well in that role-play, it was difficult but you managed it', and then follow up by saying, 'You used a gentle approach by hinting at what you wanted. An alternative to what you did would have been to have asked Jimmy directly for what you wanted. That might have been more effective.'

The value of feedback can be enhanced by firstly modelling the way to give feedback and then directly teaching the children how to give feedback to each other themselves.

Using questions

Whereas questions are best used sparingly when counselling children individually, they can be very useful in group work. A range of suitable types of question from a number of different theoretical approaches can be used. Examples of these are:

Questions to heighten a child's awareness

These questions help the child to recognise and own feelings and thoughts. Examples are 'What are you feeling emotionally right now?', 'What is happening inside you right now?' and, 'What are your tears saying?'

Follow-up questions to elicit more information

Questions such as 'can you tell me more?' and 'Is there anything else you can tell me about . . . ?', are useful in encouraging children to continue in the disclosure of information which might otherwise be censored.

Circular questions

Circular questions are directed to one child, and ask that child about the thoughts or feelings of another child or other children. Thus they invite individual group members to think about other children and their behaviours, thoughts and feelings. Often the use of circular questions will promote useful discussion between children and this may enhance group cohesion. Examples of circular questions are 'Fiona, what do you think Michael feels when Alice ignores him when he is talking to her?' and 'Jack, if you had a guess, what do you think Jacob might be thinking now that he's handed over the leadership of his team to Leslie?'

Transitional questions

Transitional questions help children return to the content of a previous discussion which has been interrupted. They are particularly useful in children's groups where children easily deflect away from topics which may be difficult to talk about. Examples are 'Earlier, David, you talked about your mum and dad separating. I wonder how you feel about that right now?' and 'A while back, Sally was telling us about the time when her brother attacked her father with a knife. Has anyone else in the group had a frightening experience like that?'

Guru questions

Guru questions can empower group members to give advice and be helpful to, and supportive of, other children. These questions encourage group members to seek advice from each other rather than relying on asking a leader. An example of a Guru question is, 'Sally, imagine for a moment that you are a Guru and that you could give advice to Monica about her problem. What advice would you give her?'

At suitable times group members might be invited to volunteer to be the Guru for a particular purpose. For example, a leader might ask, 'Who would like to be a Guru to advise Bruce?' Alternatively, Bruce might be invited to seek his own solution by being asked the Guru question, 'Bruce, imagine for a moment that you were a Guru and you could give advice to someone with a problem just like yours, what advice would you give?' Such a question is particularly powerful in helping children to discover their own inner resources.

Choice questions

These questions are useful when processing the outcomes of incidents which arise in a children's group. Examples are, 'What would have been a better choice for you to have made at the time when Hannah snatched your pencil?' and 'If the same situation arises again, what do you think you will do?'

To help a child move away from an incident and become more fully integrated into the group a leader could continue by asking, 'What would you like to do now' and, 'Would you like to continue talking about what happened or would you like to move on to something new?'

Exception-oriented

Exception-oriented questions help children to recognise that they can, if they wish, think and/or behave in ways that are more helpful to themselves than the ways which cause problems for them. Exception-oriented questions draw attention to, and amplify, the non-problematic areas of a child's life by focusing on exceptions when the problem does not occur. Examples of an exception-oriented question to be used with a child who bullies others is, 'Are there times when you don't bully anyone?' and, 'When does that happen?', 'How does your day go when you don't bully anyone?' 'Who would be the first to notice if the problem didn't happen?'

Cheer-leading, accenting and amplifying questions

These questions recognise and affirm that desirable behavioural change has occurred. They make the change newsworthy so that the child receives reinforcement for the changed behaviour. These questions are particularly useful following exception-oriented questions. Examples are, 'How did you do that?', 'How did you manage to carry through that decision?', 'That's fantastic!' and, 'That must have been difficult to do. How did you do it?'

Miracle questions

These questions encourage children to focus on solutions rather than the problem. The answers from these questions often lead to ongoing discussion with the discovery of goals which are achievable. Examples are, 'If you had a magic wand and you could change what was happening, what would you be doing differently?' and 'If you had a magic wand and could change the situation, what would you see that would be different?'

Scaling questions

These questions are useful in helping children to set goals and recognise change in themselves which may occur within the group or away from the group. When using scaling questions, the whole group can be used to support the goal setting of an individual member. Examples of scaling questions are, 'On a scale of one to ten, one being as quiet as a mouse and ten being as noisy as a ferocious dinosaur, where do you think that you would fit right now?', 'Where would you like to be on the scale today?', 'What can you do to reach this point on the scale?' and, 'What can the group do to help you reach this point on the scale?'

Leader self-disclosure skills

A limited amount of self-disclosure of feelings, beliefs and opinions by group leaders can be useful in some types of children's groups. Self-disclosure by leaders allows them to be authentic and gives the group the chance to get to know them as people. It helps to create trust between group members and the leaders.

In those children's groups where self-disclosure by the children is desired, self-disclosure by leaders models appropriate behaviour. It may also enable leaders to deal directly with immediacy issues that may have been noticed by the children, but which they may be unable to verbalise. For example, a leader might disclose feelings of being distracted, by saying, 'I'm being distracted by the noise which is coming from outside, and I wonder how the group feel about it?'

The risk in overuse of self-disclosure is that the leader runs the risk of meeting his or her own needs at the expense of the needs of members of the group (Ehly and Dustin, 1989). Also, in self-disclosing, leaders do need to be sensitive to socio-economic and cultural differences between themselves and the children in the group. For example, leaders who are fortunate enough to enjoy a middle-class lifestyle may distance themselves from low socio-economic group children if they refer to their use of material possessions or their participation in activities that are not available to the children and their families.

Confrontation

At times it is necessary for leaders to be confronting. They may wish to draw a child's, or the group's, attention to incongruities between what is being said and what is being done or expressed non-verbally. They may also need to confront a child or the group with regard to unacceptable behaviour.

A rule of thumb for confrontation is that before confronting a child, a leader should try to ensure that the confrontation is done as a conscious deliberate act rather than as a knee-jerk response to unconscious triggers (Spitz, 1987). Confrontation should be designed to achieve a specific result, usually in the 'here and now'. It should be simultaneously tough and tender, in an empathic atmosphere of genuine concern and caring (Rachman and Raubolt, 1985).

PROCESSING SKILLS

Processing an activity or an interaction between members of a group involves verbally exploring what each child, and the group as a whole, experienced while engaged in the activity or interaction. Processing is an intervention that is deliberately used by a leader in order to bring into focus what has occurred in the group, and to raise the children's awareness of their emotional feelings, thoughts, opinions and beliefs with regard to what has occurred.

There are considerable advantages to be gained if leaders repeatedly, but not excessively, interrupt the normal flow of group work in order to process activities and interactions. Processing may be carried out after the completion of an activity or interaction, or sometimes an activity or interaction may be interrupted to allow for immediate processing.

Processing usually involves the use of counselling skills. What the leader does to process an activity or interaction is to ask questions and use feedback of observations to discover what emotional feelings, perceptions, thoughts, opinions and beliefs each child experienced while engaged in the activity or interaction.

Processing may also bring into the open factual information about behaviours or group and/or individual processes. Through processing children learn to take notice of their feelings and thoughts and to recognise the influence of these on their beliefs, attitudes, cognitive processes and behaviours. With this increased awareness changes in beliefs, attitudes, cognitive processes and behaviours may occur. Importantly, children may recognise the influence of behaviours, thoughts and feelings on themselves and others. This, in turn, can influence the ways they communicate and their relationships with others. Processing not only offers the means for group members to learn about themselves as individuals but also to learn about themselves as members of a group (Ehly and Dustin, 1989).

The processing of activities can be used to raise issues and topics that are relevant to a group programme. It can be used to generate material that can be explored by the group and used educationally to assist in the promotion of positive changes in individual thinking and behaviours and in inter-personal relationships.

Processing activities

A number of examples of the processing of activities will be considered. These will include the processing of art, symbolic work, games, motor activities, small group and team work. As discussed previously, activities alone are usually insufficient in themselves for the achievement of goals, but they become of immense value in this regard when processed as described above. The processing of activities makes them meaningful and allows for learning and change to take place in a climate of safety.

Processing may include consideration and discussion of how the children in a group experience, and can express their experience, of any of the following:

Group identity	Self-disclosure	Leadership	Sharing
Shared purpose	Discoveries	Organisation	Helping
Common goals	Safety	Sequencing	Conflict resolution
Rules	Exposure	Competition	Cooperation
Boundaries	Intrusion	Fairness	Dependence
Collaboration	Tolerance	Attributes	Independence
Participation	Fun	Outcomes	Problem solving
Joining	Interest	Limitations	Validation
Sense of belonging	Creativity	Support	Equality

Art and symbolic work

The most essential part of processing art or symbolic work is to give specific non-interpretive feedback about things the leader observes or notices. Leaders should invite children to explain the meaning of their work. A leader might begin by asking, 'Can you tell the group about your drawing/symbol', and then, 'Is there anything more you can tell the group about your picture'. The second question is useful as it encourages the child to think more deeply. Non-interpretive feedback from a leader may result in a child getting more fully in touch with the feelings, meanings and ideas being expressed through the work. With the child's permission, other members of the group may be invited to ask questions about, or comment on, the work.

Games and motor activities

Processing children's experience of participating in games provides an opportunity for leaders to explore the children's beliefs, attitudes, thoughts and feelings as they arise in response to the activity. These beliefs, attitudes, thoughts and feelings are likely to be related to the children's constructs with regard to interpersonal relationships. Issues such as turn taking, cheating, fairness, skill level, intimidation, support and encouragement can be explored.

Suitable questions a leader might ask to facilitate the processing of a game or motor activity might be:

- How did you feel inside when we . . . (played drakes and dragons)?
- What do you think Leslie could have done differently?
- What do you think happened?
- What do you think about what happened?
- What did you notice when. . . . (Bert pushed Alec)?

Small group and team work

Often small group work will involve games or activities, and these can be processed as described above. Additionally, small group and team work raises issues of collaboration, competition, cooperation and group ownership. These issues can be explored during processing. Leaders might ask question such as:

- What was it like to make the mural together?
- How did it feel to finish first?
- What was it like to be team leader?
- What was the best thing your leader did?
- If you had been the leader, what would you have done differently?
- What do you think it was like for Mary when Alice made a hole in Mary's clay shape?

To make the most of opportunities for learning and promoting change in children, it is preferable if most, if not all, group activities are processed by leaders in the way described above.

FACILITATION SKILLS

Central to a leader's role is the orchestration of the group programme in such a way that the children experience a process that has a natural and comfortable flow as they participate in meaningful activity and discussion. Leaders needs to be active, involved, responsive and sensitive to the psychosocial needs relevant to the developmental age of the children in the group. Despite the theoretical approach used, at all times support and facilitation need to be uppermost in the leader's mind.

Effective facilitation creates an atmosphere of safety and containment so that the children become free to explore, express themselves and gain from their experience. Facilitation involves giving directions and instructions, introducing and organising activities, facilitating discussion, giving support, teaching and giving advice, modelling and dealing with exits from the group.

Giving directions or instructions

When children join a group they are naturally uncertain about their leaders' expectations of them. In order to feel safe, they need to be confident that someone is in charge and that the person in charge will take control and give directions and instructions when necessary. They also need to be clear about group rules, responsibilities and issues related to confidentiality.

The way in which directions and instructions are given will depend on the theoretical orientation of the group leaders. Even so, directions need to be given simply and clearly so they are understood by children of the relevant developmental age. Often it is useful to give reasons for instructions so that children understand the purpose of the instructions. Leaders also need to check out that instructions have been understood. This may be done after giving an instruction by asking whether anyone has any questions. For some children it is useful to repeat instructions, especially where there have been interruptions while instructions are being given.

Group rules and responsibilities

Leaders are responsible for the safety and well-being of children in their groups, so must be responsible for making decisions regarding

127

group rules, making sure the children understand them and implementing them. However, it can be very helpful for group cohesion and the acceptance of rules if they are devised collaboratively with the children. In this way the leaders and the children themselves are actively involved in devising rules for the group. Individual children may then feel they are contributing to the development of the group ethos and may consequently have an increased sense of belonging.

Group rules for older children are best framed in terms of positive behaviours rather than negative ones. For example, it is preferable to make a rule, 'We will take turns to talk' instead of, 'No interrupting'. Another positive rule might be, 'We will help others to feel safe' instead of, 'Hurting other children is not allowed'. For younger children, rules need to include clear statements of both desirable and unacceptable behaviours. For example, all of the following rules may be included: 'Take turns'; 'Share'; 'Help others'; 'No snatching'; 'No pushing'; and 'No hitting'.

Rules should reinforce issues of safety, acceptance, understanding, respect, trust and appropriate behaviours around conflict resolution. Rules may be changed during the life of a group. This is preferably done through consensus and in response to unexpected events or behaviours in the group, or to address the evolving needs of the group.

Once group rules have been established, responsibility and consequences for inappropriate behaviour need to be discussed and clearly spelt out. Consequences may extend over a range from minimal to more severe. For example a consequence for breaking a rule the first time, or in a minor way, may be time out for two minutes. After further, or more serious, breaches the consequence may rise to time out for ten minutes, then to leaving the group for the rest of the session and finally, after several severe breaches, to leaving the group permanently.

Sometimes it can be useful to use a token system, where tokens are given to children when leaders notice they have been able to use behaviours consistent with the rules, or have been helpful to others or useful in achieving group goals. The tokens act as reinforcers or rewards and tend to increase the frequency of desired behaviours. Generally, whenever possible, it is preferable to use rewards rather than negative consequences. Sometimes tokens can be withheld or taken away, however, as a response cost, when undesirable behaviours need to be extinguished.

Recognising and dealing with confidentiality issues

In many children's groups the children need to be able to trust that there will be some level of confidentiality. If this is not so, they may not be willing to participate freely and to disclose information which relates to their issues. They may fear that in disclosing information about themselves or their families they are being disloyal or betraying others. They may also worry in case information they share in the group may get back to members of their family or peers.

The confidentiality issue is complicated, as parents or carers have rights to information about their children. It is therefore sensible for leaders to discuss the issue of confidentiality with parents at the assessment stage as discussed in Chapter 6.

Children have the right to disclose abusive behaviours by parents or others. If disclosed, some behaviours may have to be reported to parents/carers and/or the appropriate authorities to ensure the ongoing safety and protection of the child.

When discussing issues of confidentiality with children in a group, confidentiality limits, conditions and exceptions need to be made clear early in the group programme. This enables children to raise confidential issues while being fully aware of possible consequences.

Unfortunately, group leaders cannot ensure that children in a group will respect confidentiality. They may disclose information to peers and/or to family members. Responsible leaders may wish to explain this to their groups, and to help the group discuss the possible consequences of inappropriately shared material.

Introducing and organising activities

When activities are organised or introduced group leaders need to explain clearly what is expected. Often, some children in a group will be familiar with a particular activity, whereas others will not. When introducing activities, it is sensible to explain how the activity relates to the purpose of the group.

Some activities require particular facilitation skills. These include role plays, check-in activities and joining exercises.

Role plays

Role plays are often used in children's groups. There are two types of role play. One, where the child role plays another person in order to help him or her experience and understand interpersonal relationships and other people's perspectives, and the other where the child uses role play to practise and rehearse new behaviours. With both types of role play leaders need to encourage and coach children in their roles.

When children role play another person, they take on roles that are uncharacteristic for them. In role plays of this type it is essential for leaders to ensure that the children are satisfactorily able to move out of role, and recognise the difference between the role they were playing and themselves. Where role plays are used to help children practise and rehearse appropriate behaviours, moving out of role is unnecessary because the children need to be encouraged to continue using the practised behaviours.

In order to help children move out of role, leaders can point out that the child is not the person who was role played, and then make use of two questions. These are firstly to ask, 'In what ways are you like the person you role played?', and, secondly, after hearing the reply to the first question, 'In what ways are you different from that person?' Finally the leader can confirm that the child is him or herself.

Check-in activities

Leaders need to be familiar with the use of check-in activities so that they can introduce and use them. A number of check-in activities are included in the sample group programmes described in Chapters 10 to 13. Details of these activities are included in Appendix A. Checking in at the beginning of a group helps children to expand their boundaries. Thus they are able to move from being isolated individuals into a new position where they confirm their individuality by expressing their similarities and differences, and at the same time begin to experience a sense of belonging to the group.

Check-in activities help the children to stay in the 'here and now'. They provide an opportunity for group members to put to one side thoughts, feelings and attitudes which they had when they arrived to join the group. If they are not given an opportunity to do this, then these thoughts, feelings and attitudes might intrude on their ability to focus on the group's activities and to participate fully.

Check-in activities can also normalise and de-stigmatise beliefs, values, and attitudes, which group members might have concerning themselves.

Joining exercises

Effective facilitation requires the use of joining exercises at the beginning of group programmes to enhance the children's sense of belonging and help them to get to know each other. A number of joining activities are included in the sample group programmes described in Chapters 10 to 13. Details of these activities are included in Appendix A. Joining activities aim to help children feel free and at ease within a group. They provide an opportunity for them to experience what it feels like to be in the group, to join with other members of the group and to begin to feel the necessary sense of belonging. Joining activities also enable group members to start establishing relationships with the leaders and to begin to understand expectations relating to the group experience.

Joining activities can help children in a group to gain a sense of togetherness so that group cohesiveness can start to develop. For this to occur there needs to be agreement about group objectives, rules and boundaries, and an acceptance of the leaders and their roles.

Facilitating discussion

To facilitate discussion, leaders need to guide the verbal exchanges between and among children in a group. While facilitating discussion the leaders themselves may also participate in it. When a discussion is taking place the counselling skills described previously can be used to provide the children with the opportunity to share their thoughts, feelings and ideas on relevant topics. Leaders may need to encourage children who are not participating to contribute, and to deal with monopolising behaviour and interruptions. Leaders may also need to deal with diversions and inappropriate contributions from children. Discussions are particularly helpful if they enable children, expand on their ideas and hear varying opinions of others (O'Rourke and Worzbyt, 1996).

Giving support

Support involves helping children feel safe, respected and valued while they explore anxieties and fears. As a consequence of appropriate support from leaders, the children's self-esteem may be enhanced. Support can enable them to bridge the gap between being dependent on the leader and becoming independent from the leader. It allows them to regress when necessary without criticism. Sometimes a leader's support may be directed towards the whole group, and at other times towards some members of the group or the whole group.

Teaching and giving advice

Group leaders can teach children particular ways of thinking and behaving and can encourage the learning of associated skills during group sessions. While self-discovery has advantages, children expect leaders to be knowledgeable and to share useful information about values, beliefs, attitudes and behaviours. Children can then, if they choose, integrate these into their own thinking.

In groups, teaching and giving advice are likely to be impactful because the information is received collectively by the children, may be discussed in the group setting and reinforced through consensus. When teaching and giving advice it is important to recognise and respect that there are differences in opinions, beliefs and attitudes, culturally and socially.

Teaching is particularly important with regard to protective behaviours, coping and self-management skills, problem solving skills and rational thinking skills.

Protective behaviours

Teaching protective behaviours involves helping children to learn to look after themselves and keep themselves safe from harm and potential danger. They need to learn about appropriate boundaries and how to protect themselves from physical and emotional harm such as occurs in physical and sexual abuse.

Coping and self-management skills

Teaching coping and self-management skills involves helping children to recognise critical moments. The purpose of establishing the critical moment is to help the child recognise points in time when he or she could STOP, THINK and DO something different from what he or she has in the past usually done, with undesirable consequences.

Problem-solving skills

Leaders can teach children helpful problem-solving skills to enable them to find solutions to day-to-day problems so that they can engage in adaptive behaviours. Primary problem-solving skills include alternative thinking, consequential thinking and means–end thinking (Rose and Edleson, 1987). Alternative thinking is the ability to generate multiple solutions to problem situations. Consequential thinking is the ability to anticipate short and long term consequences of various alternative behaviours and use this information in decision making. Means–end thinking is the ability to plan a series of specific actions necessary to carry out the solution to a problem.

Rational thinking skills

Leaders can teach children to understand their own thinking patterns so that they can recognise their own self-destructive or self-defeating thought processes, challenge unhelpful messages they are giving themselves and replace these by more useful ones.

Modelling

Modelling depends on the child's ability to observe the behaviour of the leaders and/or others in the group and then to imitate it. Leaders can enhance this process by drawing attention to appropriate behaviours, and rewarding them. As a consequence, other group members may emulate the desired behaviours. Desired behaviours can also be rehearsed in role play so that they are learnt. This learning can be enhanced if feedback is received from others.

Dealing with exits from the group

Children may leave a group as a consequence of internal processes within the child, group dynamics and processes or influences from outside the group. They may leave as a consequence of a decision by the child, the parents or carers or the leaders. Sometimes the possibility that a child might leave can be avoided by the leaders being attentive and responsive to precipitating events that may have the potential to cause the child to leave.

Sometimes children leaving can be traumatic for other group members as they may believe they are to blame and consequently feel guilty. They may also feel angry towards the leaders for not offering the departed child effective help. Leaders may therefore need to deal with the fallout when a child leaves or is removed from the group and carry out reparative work with the remaining children to help them understand why a child has left or been asked to leave (Lampel, 1985).

In some cases, a group may be relieved when an extremely disruptive member is removed or leaves. Even so, leaders need to process the remaining children's feelings with regard to the exit.

Occasionally, children who have left a group will return later. Their rejoining the group needs to be acknowledged and processed.

MANAGING BEHAVIOUR

When dealing with problem behaviours, leaders need to be decisive, direct, succinct and use language the child can understand.

When a child is acting out it is not always necessary to act immediately. If time is allowed to pass other children in the group may manage the behaviour. If a leader does need to take action, the first step is to state what has been noticed about the particular behaviour and the second step is to set limits. For example, a leader might say, 'You're fighting', or, 'You're angry and being rude to Alec' and then state the rule which the group has previously made relating to the behaviour in question. Thus the leader might say, 'We will solve differences without being abusive – that's a rule', or 'We will express our anger without being rude – that's a rule'. Leaders need to be firm about such rules. Additional rules can be added gradually over a period of time, if needed.

It can be useful to have a time out cushion or chair and to explain that a child can take time out when he or she chooses. Also, a leader might ask a child to take time out when needed. When sending a child to time out the message needs to be clear but framed in a positive rather than punitive way. For example, a facilitator might say, 'Marion, you seem to be having difficulty attending to what we are doing. I'd like you to sit quietly for a while. Go and sit on the cushion over there for two minutes. I'll tell you when to come back.'

Time out should be brief and used to give children a chance to calm down before coming back into the group. Involuntary time out should only be used when all else has failed. If time out is not helping a child to calm down, then it is not working and another strategy should be tried.

Sometimes it may be necessary for a leader to deal firmly with a child. The leader may need to place a hand on the shoulder of the child or to temporarily remove a child to a quiet room. Leaders should only restrain children if absolutely necessary, and preferably after removal from the room (Lampel, 1985).

Reinforcing behaviour

Rewards and positive reinforcements should be utilised liberally throughout the life of a group. They help to build self-esteem and encourage appropriate behaviour. Praise, a nod of approval or a smile are major influences in reinforcing the behaviour of children. Additionally, the use of tokens can be a powerful incentive. Tokens may be in the form of coloured cards. These can be given out as rewards for behaviour consistent with group rules and norms. Tokens can later either be exchanged for material rewards or recorded cumulatively on a thermometer chart. The use of a chart acts as a motivator, encouraging children to earn more tokens.

Reinforcement can be given to the entire group, sub-groups or individuals. Hence leaders may use individual and/or group 'thermometers' to indicate the total number of tokens earned. Group thermometers may strengthen goals related to behaviours such as collaboration and team-work, and may enhance group cohesion.

Dealing with difficult behaviours

As discussed earlier, particularly in the storming stage of group development, it is likely that leaders will observe behaviours that are unhelpful to the group process. Obviously individual children express themselves in their own unique way. However, there are some common behaviours which tend to appear at particular times during a group's development (George and Dustin, 1988). These behaviours include being resistant, monopolising, withdrawing into silence, being manipulative and forming sub-groups.

Being resistant

The resistant group member is often angry and frustrated. While this behaviour may be tolerated in the forming stage of group development, in the storming stage it is important to emphasise and encourage appropriate group behaviour. If resistance happens in the norming stage it can be troublesome and challenging for both the leaders and other members of the group, and certainly needs to be addressed or it will interfere with the achievement of group goals.

Sometimes it is possible for a group leader to deal with resistant behaviour by describing it as frustration and/or wanting to initiate change. This may give the resistant child an opportunity to talk about what is uncomfortable for him/her, and thus to achieve some changes to enable cooperative participation to occur. If this fails, it may be necessary to firmly focus attention on group rules and responsibilities.

Monopolising behaviour

Monopolising behaviour does not usually begin early in the stages of group development, but is common once a group has become more established. When dealing with monopolising behaviour by a particular child, it can be useful to allow the behaviour to occur more than once in order to observe and clearly identify a pattern or a theme before addressing the behaviour. While observing such behaviour, the leader can look around the group to observe the non-verbal behaviour of other members. Attention can then be drawn to the impact of the monopolising behaviour on the group. The leader's goal is to help the child who is engaged in the behaviour to understand when the behaviour occurs and to explore what alternatives there might be for attaining the gains that may be achieved through the monopolising behaviour. If this goal is achieved the behaviour may cease. If monopolising behaviour continues, the leader will need to draw attention to a rule, such as, 'Everyone needs to take turns in speaking.'

Withdrawing into silence

Silent behaviour may be a result of fear, anxiety, anger or simply individual difference. It can be useful for leaders to observe silent behaviour for a while to determine whether it fits a particular pattern in response to group behaviours or activities. For some children, silent behaviour may be a passive way of expressing anger. For others, silent behaviour may reflect a high level of anxiety about being part of a group and/or about self-disclosure in a group.

Some silent children may be very involved in the group's activities, even though they are silent. If children are silent, it should not be assumed they are not learning or are uninterested in what is taking place (O'Rourke and Worzbyt, 1996). They may be participating in other ways and making use of the group experience.

Usually it is sensible for leaders to accept silent behaviour and to draw attention to this acceptance during whole group processing. With acceptance, it is possible the silent child may be able to provide some explanation for the behaviour.

Manipulative behaviour

Manipulative behaviour is often viewed as an expression of anger. Manipulative behaviour can include consistently arriving late for a group and thus drawing attention to oneself, behaving in particular ways so that other children are unable to get their needs met, and behaving in ways that continually distract the leaders from the tasks at hand. Usually the best way to deal with this behaviour is by talking about it, that is by processing it, in the whole group because it is most likely that the behaviour is annoying to some group members. By doing this the manipulative nature of the behaviour can be brought into focus, recognised for what it is, and hopefully the child in question will replace the behaviour by more appropriate behaviours.

Forming sub-groups

Sometimes sub-groups will form within the whole group. The formation of sub-groups is natural human behaviour and can be useful for those within a particular sub-group. Sub-group formation is particularly evident when working with children between the ages of nine and twelve as this behaviour is a known characteristic of children in this developmental age group. Often sub-groups will form as a response to conflict.

A primary factor influencing whole group success where there are sub-groups is the sub-group's relationship with the whole group. For optimal success, sub-groups need to join with the whole group through participation in common tasks and through a direct relationship with the group leaders. Thus leaders need to involve sub-groups in the tasks and activities of the whole group even though at times they may carry out these tasks and activities separately from the whole group. As already mentioned, the whole group may resist the formation of sub-groups in the early stages of group development but is likely to be more accepting of sub-groups in later stages of group development and may view them as productive entities.

It is important for leaders not to try to undermine sub-groups, but to recognise their existence and observe their impact on the remainder of the group. Acceptance of a sub-group can be made by deliberately utilising the sub-group in team activities. This may help individual members in the group talk openly about belonging to a sub-group.

Dealing with persistent behaviours

The persistence of undesirable behaviours may be an indication that the child in question is unable to meet group norms and expectations and is having difficulty adjusting. Leaders need to re-assess whether the child is able to benefit from participation in the group. They also need to consider whether this can be done without disrupting the programme to the detriment of other children. After re-assessment it may be decided that it is in the child's and/or the group's best interests for the child to leave the group. If this is the case the child and parent/s or carer/s need to be presented with other options.

9 Evaluating the outcomes of a group programme

Research studies relating to the outcomes of group work suggest that children can derive considerable therapeutic benefit and demonstrate improved psychosocial functioning as a result of their group experiences (Grayston and De-Luca, 1995; Hoag and Burlingame, 1997; Howarth and Riester, 1997; Rose, S.R., 1998). However, this does not mean that all groups will necessarily be able to achieve their defined objectives. In order to be accountable, therefore, it is desirable that group leaders take specific action to evaluate the outcomes of their group programmes.

There are two major ways of evaluating group programmes (Rose, S.R., 1998). The first uses a form of continuous assessment and the second measures change, on particular dimensions, which has occurred over the whole life of the programme.

Evaluation through continuous assessment relies predominantly on informal data gathering and involves using a planned ongoing tracking process. This provides the opportunity for leaders to detect and correct significant deviations between group goals and actual outcomes in a timely fashion (O'Rourke and Worzbyt, 1996). This style of evaluation is highly recommended because of its ability to positively influence a programme while it is in progress so that desired outcomes are achieved.

The other common method used to evaluate a group programme is to measure relevant variables for individual children before the programme starts and after the programme finishes. The pre- and post-programme results can then be used to measure change in individual children and to determine whether the programme has achieved its goals.

The method to be used in evaluating a group programme needs to be selected during the initial programme planning stage. Then, if data needs to be collected at the beginning, or during, the programme arrangements can be made for this. In the initial planning stage the type of information to be collected must also be identified. For example, data to be collected may reflect children's individual behaviour, cognitions and/or emotions, and/or the influence of the group experience on the children.

EVALUATION OF A PROGRAMME USING PRE- AND POST-MEASURES

This method is often selected because it requires a minimum of effort from leaders. A significant limitation of this method, however, is that changes identified in the children cannot necessarily be attributed to the group programme. Outcomes may not be due to the group process itself, but may be a consequence of confounding variables such as the child spending time away from the family while attending the group, maturation and changes to the child's social system. Thus, unless leaders carry out well-planned research studies using control groups, care needs to be taken in attributing outcomes to the group process.

If group leaders accept they may not be able to conclusively prove with scientific accuracy that their groups are effective, they may still wish to look for evidence suggesting the possibility that their programmes are effective. Using pre- and post-measures can provide this evidence.

Because leaders have direct experience and involvement with their group programmes, they are likely to get strong indications from their own personal impressions regarding effectiveness. However, these indications will be subjective and need some level of confirmation through the collection of relevant data. Therefore data collected through a systematic and formal process can be useful in complementing informal and anecdotal evidence, as well as providing a more objective evaluation of group work.

In carrying out evaluation of group programmes leaders need to have a wide enough vision to be able to recognise unexpected changes which may not have been included in the group objective and goals. For example, consider a programme where a goal is to help children integrate appropriate social skills into their daily lives. It may be that this goal does not appear to have been achieved when pre- and post-measures are compared. Yet an improvement in the children's general behaviour may have been reported by their families. This would be consistent with the programme having had a useful outcome. Sometimes an additional post-measure taken several weeks after the conclusion of a programme might be used, to give an indication of the likely the effectiveness of the programme in the long term.

When evaluating a group programme using pre- and post-measures either formal or informal assessment processes may be involved. These processes may involve the child, the parents or carers and/or significant others.

CONTINUOUS EVALUATION OF A PROGRAMME

Continuous evaluation of a programme aims to improve practice through phases of planning, action, observation and reflection that lead to revised planning in the particular context in which action is occurring (Carr and Kemmis, 1986). In the continuous evaluation method, the programme is continually evaluated and may be continually revised.

The continuous evaluation method is illustrated in Figure 9.1. Once the programme has been planned, data is collected during the initial assessment process before the programme starts, as shown on the circle in Figure 9.1. This data is evaluated and the programme as initially planned is then adjusted, if necessary, in light of the data. After each session is completed, data is collected, evaluated and adjustments to the programme are made. As the programme continues, the circular process shown in Figure 9.1 is continually repeated so that effective adjustments to the programme can be made in response to the group's needs. At the conclusion of the programme, data is once again collected to obtain a final evaluation of the success of the whole programme. If the programme is to be repeated, information from the final collection of data can be used to enable leaders to revise the programme so it will be more effective when used again.

Continuous evaluation usually involves the use of informal assessment. Leaders need to allow time to collect, evaluate and make use of data to amend the programme. Data may be collected in several different ways:

1. Leaders may make notes after each session to describe and/or rate the emotional effect, behaviours, personal attributes and/or other qualities of each child.
2. Parent/s or carer/s may be invited, at various stages of the group programme, to complete questionnaires or rating scales concerning their children's current emotional state and/or behaviours.

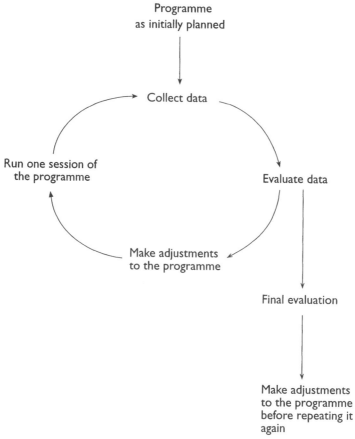

Figure 9.1   The continuous evaluation method

3. Anecdotal information from parent/s or carer/s may be collected and recorded.
4. Children in the group may be asked to provide feedback concerning their responses to group sessions.
5. During debriefing, leaders and co-leaders may discover useful information.

FORMAL AND INFORMAL DATA GATHERING

Measuring change involves collecting data using either formal or informal methods. Formal methods usually involve the use of standardised or normed assessment instruments, whereas informal methods are more qualitative and rely on the subjective judgements of significant persons and/or the clinical judgement of the leaders.

Informal data gathering

Informal methods of data gathering often target generalised performance and behaviours. They involve gathering useful information obtained through clinical observation and/or discussion, and through the questioning of significant people in the child's life. For example, leaders might ask school and community service personnel about their perceptions of change in the child. The key to successful informal data gathering is to ask the right questions. Ideas expressed by those providing information are then categorised and collated so the collected data can be evaluated.

Informal data gathering may involve writing reports of sessions in which the leaders subjectively rate behaviours of the group and individual children, and then record and report information concerning processes and outcomes. Self-reports and paper and pencil tests completed by the children may also be included. Informal data gathering may involve use of self-report questionnaires such as in Figures 9.2, 9.3 and 9.4. These can be used to get feedback from children in a group following a group session. The examples given in Figures 9.2 to 9.4 each demand a different style of response and cater for differing levels of literacy.

Informal evaluation may also include carrying out individual interviews with the children or family interviews. Sometimes such interviews can be highly structured to obtain quantitative information. This makes it possible to conduct studies which include comparative or control groups (Barry and von-Baeyer, 1997; Blonk et al., 1996; Tonkins and Lambert 1996).

The data collected can be used to indicate not only changes in individuals, but also variables relating to the whole group, such as group cohesion and satisfaction with group processes, as reported by individual members.

Formal assessment methods

Formal assessment tools must be relevant for the children and their presenting problems (Rose and Edleson, 1987). For example, the

Figure 9.2   Session evaluation form

YOUR THOUGHTS ABOUT THIS SESSION ARE REALLY IMPORTANT

My contribution to this session:

1	2	3	4	5	6	7	8	9	10

I hardly opened my mouth   I really talked a lot

How much I wanted to be involved in this session:

1	2	3	4	5	6	7	8	9	10

Not at all   Lots and lots

How much I actually was involved in this session:

1	2	3	4	5	6	7	8	9	10

Not at all   Lots and lots

I found this session:

1	2	3	4	5	6	7	8	9	10

Bored me silly   Was very interesting

Compared to others:

1	2	3	4	5	6	7	8	9	10

I had no information at all   I knew more than everybody else

Figure 9.3   Session evaluation form

Piers–Harris Children's Self Concept Scale (Piers and Harris, 1984) might be used to assess children with self-esteem problems, the Revised Children's Manifest Anxiety Scale (Reynolds and Richmond, 1985) might be used for children with high levels of anxiety and the Adaptive Behavior Assessment System (Harrison and Oakland, 2000) might be used with children who are intellectually challenged.

The validity and reliability of instruments used must be considered, together with practical constraints regarding their use.

Formal evaluation can give a useful indication of group outcomes and the effectiveness of a programme. This type of evaluation tends to be more precise than informal assessment because the results are generally quantitative. Formal assessment instruments are available for

Which activity did you find the most interesting?

....

Why? ....

Which activity did you find the least interesting?

....

Why? ....

**Do you think you have changed because of your
involvement in the activities during the session?**

....

Explain you answer here ....

....

Did you learn any skills to help you? ....

What were they? Write them here ....

....

Figure 9.4 Session evaluation form

measuring a wide range of personality, mood, behavioural, physical and mental health conditions. A list of some commonly used assessment instruments, with brief descriptions, is provided in Figure 6.1. It should be noted that some of the assessments listed are restricted for use by professionals with specific training.

The simplest way to use formal assessments to measure changes in children in a group with regard to particular criteria is to compare pre- and post-measures. A more rigorous approach involves the use of comparison between changes in children in the group undergoing the programme and changes in similar children who are not in the programme.

ASSESSMENT OF COST EFFECTIVENESS

There is considerable evidence from research studies that working with children in groups is effective for many purposes. Groups for children have been shown to be effective for children where parents have divorced (Cole and Kammer, 1984; Farmer and Galaris, 1993; Hoffman, 1984; Pedro-Carroll *et al.*, 1992), for children with self-esteem problems (Blonk *et al.*, 1996; Richert, 1986; Romano *et al.*, 1995), for children who have Attention Deficit Hyperactivity Disorder (Lock, 1996), for children suffering emotional trauma (Kopala and Keitel, 1998; Trounson, 1996), for children with problem solving skills and social skills difficulties (Rose, S.R., 1985, 1986), and for children with school performance problems (Hess *et al.*, 1990).

Although groups for children have been conclusively demonstrated to be effective, little research evidence to date has been published to compare the cost effectiveness of working with children in groups with the cost effectiveness of using other alternatives. Leaders who deem it sensible to run groups often find they are required by funding bodies, senior management or administrative personnel to justify the use of group work for children with regard to its cost effectiveness. Evaluation of cost effectiveness may also be required in agencies and government departments as a part of accreditation procedures.

It needs to be acknowledged that running groups for children does involve the expenditure of human and material resources. Consequently, in order to meet the requirements of accountability it is appropriate for estimates of cost effectiveness to be determined. Ehly and Dustin (1989) suggest that group counselling is not necessarily more economical in time than individual work. They point out that in group work there is time spent in planning, a very real need to consult with colleagues (and a supervisor), and the possibility of increased requests for individual time from members of the group. Thus group leaders may not actually save time by running groups instead of counselling children individually.

When calculating cost for each child involved in a group programme, leaders need to take into account those costs listed in Chapter 4. The cost per child can then be compared with the cost per child required to bring about similar gains using other approaches such as individual work, the use of parenting programmes or family therapy.

When making cost comparisons, it needs to be recognised that some types of change may not be achievable in any other way except by using group work. For example, it is difficult, if not impossible, to teach social skills without a context of social interaction. Consequently, for this purpose group work may be the only practical method available and cost comparisons are irrelevant.

Another factor that needs to be considered relates to the duration of the effects of group work when compared with other approaches.

It may be that changes produced through working with children in groups have a longer term effect than changes produced by other methods. Unfortunately, to date, little research has been carried out to confirm this. A further consideration relates to attrition rates; it would be interesting to compare the frequency with which children drop out of group work with the drop-out rate for individual work.

ASSESSMENT OF LEADERSHIP STYLE AND MODEL OF PRACTICE

Leaders have an ethical responsibility to the children they work with, and their parent/s or carer/s, to determine the effectiveness, usefulness and limits of the methods they use. It can be particularly advantageous if the evaluation of a group programme includes information relating to the leaders' effectiveness, because this information can enable them to improve their performance.

Running groups can make heavy demands on leaders in terms of work-load and emotional energy, so in evaluating leaders' performance it is essential to ensure that the processes used are as non-threatening as possible. If this is not the case, leaders may have good cause to fear that evaluation outcomes may have negative consequences for them. Because of this, many group leaders prefer self-evaluation. Unfortunately, such evaluations are susceptible to denial of inadequacies and limitations.

Evaluation of leadership styles and models of practice provides the most effective means for leaders to discover ways to develop their skills, modify their leadership behaviours and amend their management of group processes. Systematic, ongoing and formalised feedback that reveals the effective aspects of a programme can be very useful in this regard.

Leaders who, in the planning stage, purposefully include processes to evaluate their practice, have the potential to uncover rewarding information. When designing evaluation processes for assessing the impact of leadership style and practice on group outcomes, a solution-focused approach is preferred as this approach seeks to determine possibilities for improvement in group leadership, instead of focusing on the negative aspects of leadership. Evaluation methods used might be included in debriefing and supervision.

Debriefing

Debriefing following each group session, as described in Chapter 7, can provide a useful starting point from which to begin an evaluation of the impact of leadership style and practice on group outcomes. Debriefing might include an evaluation of surveys or check-lists completed by the children to determine whether they identify activities that were useful in achieving goals.

If a leader identifies a particular area of leadership practice which he or she wants to improve, specific feedback regarding the leader's performance in that area may be requested from a co-leader or supervisor. For example, during debriefing it might be noted that there was an increase in the amount of advice given as compared with facilitated problem-solving. The leader might seek feedback and decide to implement strategies to change this in the next session.

Supervision

Supervision, as described in Chapter 7, can include the use of direct observation by a supervisor through a video link or one-way mirror. For the specific purposes of evaluating the practice of leaders, this method of supervision combined with reflective team processes as described by Andersen (1991) can be useful. The aim of using reflective team processes is to extend and expand the work of the group leader.

The following guidelines, from reflective team processes, have been found useful in helping supervisors give feedback in an acceptable form that is most likely to produce improvement in practice:

1. Observations need to be discussed in terms of instances of achievement or demonstrated resourcefulness.
2. It is useful if exceptions to difficulties are identified so that leaders recognise strengths rather than focusing on weaknesses.
3. Possible next steps towards improvement in practice can be explored.
4. Stories, themes and metaphors can be used to enable the leader to consider other perspectives.
5. The supervisor's language should avoid pressure to produce only one solution and give an invitation to explore other possibilities. For example, a supervisor might make statements such as,

'What impressed me was . . .', 'I wondered how (Johnny) was able to . . .', 'One issue that seemed to emerge was . . .', and 'I had a picture of . . . when the discussion was taking place'.
6. Particular discussion around critical incidents can be helpful in the leader's discovery of alternatives.

CONCLUSION

It can be useful to gather a range of complementary information when evaluating outcomes of group work (Rose, S.R., 1998). A combination of quantitative and qualitative methodologies can be used. Informal information regarding individual group members, the leaders' style, parent and other community perceptions and sessional and whole programme outcomes can give leaders and the organisations which employ them useful information regarding the success of group work with children.

PART IV

GROUP PROGRAMMES FOR PARTICULAR PURPOSES

Introduction

The programmes described in Chapters 10 to 13 are examples of programmes for various types of group. They reflect a variety of theoretical approaches and differ from each other in their overall design.

Each of the programmes has been designed in accordance with the process described in Chapter 5. They all include a combination of activities, media and discussion in order to maintain the interest of the children, and have been used successfully with relevant target groups. It cannot be assumed, however, that without modification, they will necessarily be suitable for all children in a particular target group. While these programmes can be generally suitable, leaders may need to modify them to take account of the specific and individual needs of the children they intend to include in their groups. These specific and individual needs may be identified by reviewing data obtained during the initial assessment stage (see Chapter 6) as well as later once the programme is running. The programmes have been designed for specific age groups and will require modification if they are used for different age groups.

All activities, games, video tapes and work-books referred to in Chapters 10 to 13 are described in Appendix A, and relevant worksheets are either referenced in the text or in Appendix B. Where session programmes indicate that processing is to occur following an activity or game, this should be carried out as described in Chapter 8 with the aim of promoting the goals of the session.

	Table 10.1	Group programmes	
Chapter	**Target group**	**Type of group**	**Theoretical approach**
10	Children from families where violence has occurred	Counselling and psycho-educational	Integrative
11	Children with Attention Deficit Hyperactivity Disorder	Developmental skills and psycho-educational	Cognitive behavioural and behavioural
12	Children with low self-esteem	Counselling and personal growth	Experiential and post-modern
13	Children who have difficulty with social skills	Psycho-educational	Cognitive behavioural

10 Domestic violence programme

This chapter describes a programme for children, aged nine to twelve years, who come from families where violence has occurred. The programme consists of ten one-and-a-half hour sessions held at weekly intervals. Children wishing to join this programme need to be assessed as described in Chapter 6.

The programme is suitable for continuous evaluation, with outcomes being evaluated according to the achievement of session goals as listed at the beginning of individual session programmes. The overall programme assumes the group will be run primarily as a counselling and psycho-educational group. A pro-active leadership style is recommended (see Chapter 7).

THE WEEKLY PROGRAMME

The programme was planned on the basis of assumptions, as listed in Chapter 3, about children who have come from families where there has been violence. The first session is to be attended by parents without their children and the remaining sessions by the children without their parents. Session topics are as follows:

1. Parent information group
2. Joining and getting to know you
3. Defining abuse and violence
4. Breaking the secret and talking about abuse
5. Sharing experiences
6. Understanding abuse is not okay under any circumstances
7. Understanding that it is okay to be angry and learning how to ask to get needs met without being aggressive
8. Attributing responsibility for parental violence to the adult/s involved
9. Feeling safe and having fun
10. Saying 'Goodbye'

Week one – parent information group

Goals

To help the parents recognise that the programme is intended to meet their children's needs and to inform them of the goals it aims to achieve. To join with the parents, help them to understand how the programme will be run and help them feel comfortable about their children being in the group.

The programme for parents:

2.00pm Joining activity – give the following instructions, one at a time:

● Without talking line up in order of your birthday
● You might want to check with the person on either side of you if you are in the right place for your birth date
● Turn to the person on your left, introduce yourself, and share three things about yourself which you don't mind them knowing (the leader models this)

When all the participants have introduced themselves and shared information, invite the parents to return to their seats. Then invite them to introduce themselves, one by one, and to share one thing about themselves with the whole group.

Process this exercise by asking questions such as:

● How do you feel now?
● How did you feel when you were doing the exercise?
● What was it like doing the exercise?
● Is there anything you would have liked to have done differently?

Tell the parents that the same method of processing will be used, after activities, with children in the group.

2.30pm Give the parents the following information:

1. The content and topics for each weekly session of the children's programme.
2. The goals of the programme: to empower the children to break the secret of family violence, to teach them that abuse is not OK, to

teach them safe non-violent ways of relating and to improve their self-esteem.

3. Information about the issues that are likely to be relevant for the children in the group as a consequence of their experiences and ages.

Explain how weekly topics will be explored through the use of games, discussion, activities, and videos. Discuss the importance of the snack (see Chapter 3). Ask parents if there are any restrictions which need to be placed on food or drink for their children.

Information about important issues for the children will include the following:

- Children within this age group focus on social contacts away from family and home. Therefore it is important for them to realise that most other families live without conflict.
- Victimisation and misuse of power may have distorted the children's beliefs and concepts regarding male/female relationships, roles and self-image.
- Poor modelling, trauma and internal conflicts are likely to have affected social relationships.
- The children may have difficulty with conflicting loyalty.
- Issues of gender, self-identity and personal values are made easier in the context of successful family relationships.
- Talking about emotional issues is likely to be difficult for the children.
- Conflict resolution without resorting to violence needs to be learnt.

3.00pm Discuss issues relating to possibly informing non-custodial parents that their children will be attending the group. In instances where children still have contact with a non-custodial parent there may be a need for that parent to be informed about the child's participation in the group, or there may be problems for the child. Informing the non-custodial parent (where the child still has contact with that parent) can be useful in:

- Enabling the child to break the secret
- Helping the child avoid experiencing feelings of guilt for breaking family secrets
- Avoiding unpleasant or dangerous repercussions if the non-custodial parent finds out, in some other way, that the child is attending the group

Discuss options including:

- The custodial parent might want to inform the other parent themselves
- The custodial parent might ask the agency to write to the other parent to inform them (not to seek consent)
- The non-custodial parent might be invited to talk to the leader of the group by phoning the agency

3.30pm Afternoon tea

Week two – joining

Goals

To help the children get to know each other, to become aware of the purpose of the group and its format and content, to establish group rules and to have fun.

The programme

2.00pm Use the 'balloon game' to provide an opportunity for the children to introduce themselves to each other.

2.15pm Process the balloon game highlighting issues of getting to know each other and having fun.

2.20pm Have a whole group discussion using children's books on domestic violence. This is to help explain the purpose of the group and share with the group the topics to be covered during the programme.

2.35pm Play the team game 'crows and cranes' to provide an opportunity for fun and to help build group cohesion. Then process the game in terms of fun and group cohesion.

2.45pm In the whole group, set group rules, responsibilities, and consequences, so that a safe and supportive group environment will be created.

3.00pm Photographic session. Take a photograph of each child that can be developed for use in a later session.

157

3.15pm Snack.

3.30pm Close.

Materials needed for this session

Sticky name tags, masking tape, books, camera, film, cardboard, felt pens, coloured balloons, tape recorder, tape of suitable music, and refreshments.

Week three – defining abuse and violence

Goals

To help the children to feel comfortable talking about abuse, to learn basic definitions of violence and abuse, to learn that abuse is not okay under any circumstances and that provocation does not justify abuse.

The programme

2.00pm Check-in using the group activity 'pass the ball' to provide an opportunity for the children to reintroduce themselves to the whole group and begin to share with the group how they feel.

2.10pm Whole group activity: revise the rules. This is to re-acquaint members of the group with the rules, responsibilities and consequences of belonging to the group.

2.20pm Whole group activity defining abuse using the 'abuse continuum'. This activity will then be processed to facilitate each child's understanding of abusive behaviour and to discriminate between vandalism, abuse, etc.

2.30pm Discuss coping with bullying using the work-sheet 'Biffin the bully' (Geldard and Geldard, 1997), working individually with the children. This is a work-sheet designed to help children label abusive behaviour encountered in situations of bullying. Clearly, even though abuse at any level is not okay, some abusive behaviour is not as severe as other abusive behaviour. Using this work-sheet the child is invited to plot abusive behaviours on a continuum from least serious to most serious. The child's attention can then be drawn to the fact that all of the abusive behaviours have been plotted within the international symbol which signifies 'not permitted'. A strong message is therefore given that all abusive behaviour is unacceptable no matter how minor it may be. Although the abusive behaviours are attributed to Biffin the bully, the child is invited to consider the possibility that Biffin may change, hence the child may be encouraged to see that it is the behaviour and not the person who is to be criticised.

2.35pm Process the work-sheet to encourage the children to begin recognising and sharing their own personal experiences of abuse and violence.

2.40pm Whole group game, 'name steps'. This is to provide an opportunity for each child to experience being in control and to practise some leadership qualities. Follow with processing around issues of control, relating the control of one's own abusive behaviour.

2.50pm Use the activity 'secrets' with the whole group. Process this to provide an opportunity for group members to normalise their experiences, and to understand and gain feedback about abusive behaviours they may have used in the past.

3.00pm Whole group sharing of personal experiences of violence and abuse within the family home. This is to provide an opportunity for sharing and expression of feelings related to living in a home where there is violence.

3.15pm Snack

3.30pm Close

Materials needed for this session

A ball, paper, felt pens, butcher's paper for the continuum work-sheets and refreshments.

Week four – breaking the secret and talking about abuse

Goals

To confront the range of feelings produced by the experience of violence, to know there are other families who have experienced and experience violence, to feel less different from children in other families and to be less ashamed of one's own family.

The programme

2.00pm Check in using the 'pick a face' method, to provide the children in the group with an opportunity to focus on the 'here and now', to recognise how they feel at the present time and to reconnect with the purpose of the group. Pay special attention to the children's emotional state at check-in, and give them time to process any emotionally loaded issues before moving on to showing the video.

2.10pm Be familiar with the video before showing it to the children because it is powerful. Play the video-tape entitled 'It's not always happy at my house' (running time 33 minutes), or for older children, 'Crown Prince', running time 38 minutes. During the film watch the children's reactions and if necessary give them verbal affirmation and support.

2.45pm Process the video by inviting the children to discuss the video and their reactions to it. This is to integrate themes from previous group discussions (or example, definitions of abuse, and feelings and attitudes about violence) and to allow the children to compare their own experiences with those of the children in the video.

3.00pm Play the team game 'Newspaper hockey' to raise the group's energy and promote a mood change.

3.15pm Snack

3.30pm Close

Materials needed for this session

Video-tape, 'It's not always happy at my house', VCR and monitor, two rolled up newspapers, two newspaper balls, facial expression cards, and refreshments.

Week 5 – sharing experiences

Goals

To help the group share personal and family experiences related to violence and to experience the accompanying feelings, to know that other children in the group have also experienced violence in the home and to feel less different and less ashamed of one's own family.

The programme

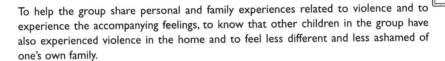

2.00pm Use the 'weather chart' check-in activity.

2.10pm Individual activity: Art. Draw your worst experience. Provide soft background music to create a pleasant atmosphere to enable the children to concentrate on their drawings. This is to provide an opportunity for the children to get in touch with and express feelings tied to traumatic experiences.

2.25pm Process the activity with regard to remembering unpleasant experiences. Explore whether memories of these intrude at times and how the memories make the children feel now. During processing, support and encourage the children but do not push them to talk about things they are not ready to share with the group.

2.40pm Play the game 'sardines' in the whole group. Process the activity in terms of hiding from others, and then joining with others. Draw a parallel between being ashamed of the family and then finding a group of children who have had similar experiences.

2.50pm Working in pairs, use the drawing activity 'What hands can do' to provide an opportunity for the children to share personal experiences of helpful and unhelpful events in their lives.

3.10pm Process the day's activities.

3.15pm Snack.

3.30pm Close.

Materials needed for this session

Paints, paper, felt pens, crayons, pencils, tape recorder and tape, or CD player, CD, and refreshments.

Week 6 – understanding that abuse is not okay in any circumstances

Goals

To address distorted values regarding violence in society, to explore issues of bullying and victimisation, to discuss the pressures and responsibilities arising from provocative behaviour of others and to explore strategies for self-control.

The programme

2.00pm Check-in using the 'choose a symbol' method. Invite the children to each choose a symbol that reflects how they are feeling and to share this with the whole group.

2.15pm Use the 'make me laugh' activity, in pairs, to help the children experience the pressures of provocation and experiment with self-control. Process this activity in terms of behaviours and actions that were used to provoke the partner's laughter.

2.30pm Play the team game 'Tweedle Dee and Tweedle Dum' to provide an opportunity for the children to experiment with and practise self-control behaviours. Process this in terms of personal space and provocation.

2.45pm Whole group discussion around behaviours within the family which can be identified as provoking behaviours, and those behaviours which can be identified as self-control behaviours.

3.00pm Play the game 'Spotto' to provide the opportunity for children to experience exercising physical control. Process this in terms of exercising physical control which may be needed when responding to provocation.

3.15pm Snack.

3.30pm Close.

Materials needed for this session

A variety of small objects to be used as symbols, and refreshments.

Week 7 – understanding that it is okay to be angry and learning to ask for needs to be met in appropriate ways

Goals

To recognise that everyone has strengths and to identify personal strengths, to know the difference between being strong and being abusive, to learn that all feelings including 'bad ones' need to be acknowledged and felt, to feel safe expressing uncomfortable feelings in the group, to recognise one's own expression of anger and to differentiate between appropriate and inappropriate expressions of anger.

The programme

2.00pm Check in using the 'draw a feeling' method.

2.15pm In small groups use the 'iceberg activity' to help children understand the concept of polarities in feelings and how feelings can shift.

2.30pm Individual activity using the work-book 'I wish the hitting would stop' (Patterson, 1990). Use the section on feelings and self-esteem. Process the activity to help the children discover the helpful aspects of thinking positively and feeling good about themselves.

2.45pm Individual activity using the 'volcano' work-sheet (Geldard and Geldard, 1997) to help the children discover the ways in which they express their anger. This work-sheet is specifically targeted at the expression of anger. When using this work-sheet each point on the volcano is discussed. For example, once the children have identified what kinds of things make them angry, they may look at the bottom of the volcano, where sitting on angry feelings can be imagined. They can then be encouraged to talk about what it would be like to sit on angry feelings, what might happen if they did and what this might be like for other people. They could be asked whether they could identify other children or people who sit

163

on their anger. Moving up the volcano to the level where anger is allowed to ooze out provides an opportunity for the children to explore a different way of expressing anger. Once again, the kinds of behaviours they might see in others when they let their anger ooze out can be identified. At the top of the volcano is the explosive angry reaction. Here the children are encouraged to examine the appropriateness and inappropriateness of this kind of expression of anger.

2.55pm Use the whole group activity the 'red balloon game' to provide an opportunity for the children to discuss the impact expressing anger has on others. Process this activity as a metaphor for anger management.

3.15pm Snack.

3.30pm Close.

Materials needed for this session

Small pieces of expanded polystyrene (subject to safety considerations), marbles, pens, two or three buckets of water, red balloons, work-sheets, work-books, and refreshments.

Week 8 – attributing responsibility for parental violence

Goals

To learn that no one deserves abuse and that domestic violence is never the child's fault, to share some personal experiences related to the violence at home, to differentiate between a person and his/her behaviour (for example, it's okay to love a parent while condemning the behaviour) and to learn that people are responsible for their behaviour and can change if they want to.

The programme

2.00pm Check in by inviting the children to express their current feelings in the form of clay shapes. Use this exercise to illustrate the concept of changing feelings by inviting the children to change their clay shapes.

2.20pm Invite the children to make sock puppets. Ask them to work in threes. In each triad, one child is to make a sock puppet in the form of a mouse, the second child is to make a sock puppet in the form of a dragon and the third child is to make a sock puppet in the form of a wizard.

2.40pm Each triad is to perform a short play, using the puppets, where the dragon and mouse fight and then end the fight. The wizard is then asked to find an alternative solution which will not lead to the negative outcomes of the fight. Process this exercise in a way which will give the children an opportunity to relate some personal experiences of violence in their homes and to explore alternative solutions to those which produced negative outcomes.

3.00pm Play the group game 'man the lifeboat' to provide an opportunity for physical expression and fun.

3.15pm Snack.

3.30pm Close.

Materials needed for this session

Clay, old clean socks, double sided adhesive tape, self-adhesive velcro, felt pieces of various colours, lace, tinsel, other decorative fabrics, large cardboard boxes to be used to make stages, and refreshments.

Week 9 – feeling safe and having fun

Goals

To identify places to go and people to call in dangerous situations, to learn how to use the telephone when calling the police or other people to get help and to identify an individual safety plan.

The programme

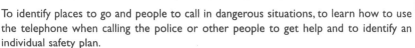

2.00pm Check in using the 'weather chart'.

2.10pm Individual activity using the work-book 'I wish the hitting would stop'. This workbook is for children living in violent homes. Share and process the activity to encourage the children to identify the difficulties of keeping safe and to explore a safety plan.

2.20pm Use the 'safety plan hand' to help the children identify their own personal safety network.

2.30pm Help the children make personal identification cards by using the 'Personal Protection ID Card' work-sheet. Use the individual photographs taken in session 1 to stick onto the ID cards. Encourage the children to list on the cards the names and phone numbers of safe places and people. The children can then keep their cards with them at all times, if that is deemed to be sensible.

2.45pm Play the game 'hotspots'. Process the game to encourage the children to understand the importance of trust, safety and accurate communication.

3.00pm Group discussion, followed by role plays and practice in using telephones to dial for help.

3.15pm Snack.

3.30pm Close.

Materials needed for this session

Weather chart, work booklet, photographs, paper plates, blindfolds, toy phones (or old phones), used phone cards, money, and refreshments.

Week 10 saying 'goodbye'

Goals

To help the children receive affirmation about themselves, to summarise the group experience, to explore ways to help other children to break the secret and to say 'goodbye'.

The programme

2.00pm Check in using the 'pick a face' method.

2.15pm Free play with craft materials during which the leaders talk with the children about the group. This can be done individually, in pairs or in small groups.

2.45pm Play the team game 'newspaper hockey'.

3.00pm Whole group discussion about the complete programme. Process this in terms of usefulness for 'other children'.

3.15pm Snack time.

3.30pm Close.

Materials needed for this session

Craft materials, rolled up newspapers, newspaper balls, face cards, and refreshments.

11 ADHD programme

This chapter describes a programme for children who have been diagnosed as having Attention Deficit Hyperactivity Disorder (ADHD). The topics for the programme are based on assumptions about children who have ADHD. The assumptions are that these children may have the following problems as identified by Nash (1994) and Wallace (1996):

- Difficulty with concentration
- Poor impulse control
- Difficulty with gratification delay
- Difficulty adjusting to transitions (from one activity to another)
- Poor receptive and expressive language skills
- Poor self-esteem
- Poor short-term memory
- Difficulty relaxing easily
- Difficulty with planning time
- Difficulty with visual and auditory memory
- Difficulty with organisation
- Difficulty with attending
- Difficulty with self-control
- Difficulty expressing feelings appropriately
- Poor social skills (including many of the items listed under social skills in Chapter 9)
- Difficulty in responding to rules and requests (especially in the presence of competing stimuli)
- Difficulty in carrying out various tasks (because poor self-control of behaviour affects ability)
- Poor motivation
- Lower than normal responsiveness to incentives and rewards
- Varying performance and effort when performing familiar tasks
- Difficulty in rejecting or blocking out distractions
- Poor interpretation of information
- Difficulty in starting or initiating important tasks or activities
- Lack of persistence or difficulty in sustaining effort
- Difficulty in completing tasks or projects

- Poor muscle coordination
- Learning problems
- Aggressive behaviours
- Inconsistent presentation of behaviours

THE PROGRAMME

This group programme is designed for use in a school setting with ADHD children of six to eight years of age. The programme is intended to be run for one hour on eight consecutive days and to replace the normal school timetable between 10am and 11am. Therefore, the children involved need to be given time away from classroom activities in order to participate. Where some activities work well they may be integrated into the regular classroom routine to help the individual child. Children joining the programme need to be assessed, as described in Chapter 6, prior to being accepted to join the group.

The programme has been designed as a closed group programme, but some children may be encouraged to repeat the programme several times to reinforce the learning of appropriate strategies. If desired, the programme can be modified to suit an open group format so that children can join and leave the programme at any stage. When using an open group format, parent information groups need to be held from time to time, with sessions three to seven being continually repeated in sequence.

This programme is suitable for pre- and post-test evaluation methods (see Chapter 9), with outcomes being evaluated according to the achievement of listed session goals. The programme assumes the group will be run primarily as a developmental skills and psycho-educational group. It has an emphasis on using a behavioural approach to reinforce the acquisition and maintenance of new behaviours. Because of the nature of Attention Deficit Hyperactivity Disorder, the leadership style will need to be pro-active with a tendency towards being authoritarian.

In this programme the skill of processing is used sparingly, because the conversational skills used in processing are demanding for ADHD children who may have difficulty with receptive and expressive language and conversational skills.

The first session of the programme is to be attended by parents without their children and the remaining sessions by the children without their parents. The daily programme is as follows:

1. Parent information group
2. Joining
3. Listening and following instructions
4. Turn taking and social interaction
5. Transitions
6. Visual memory, auditory memory and sequencing
7. Organisation and planning
8. Self-esteem and saying 'goodbye'

Day 1 – parent information group

Session goals

To describe the difficulties experienced by children with ADHD, to help parents explore their perceptions of their children who have ADHD and to familiarize them with the children's programme.

The programme for parents

10.00am Talk to the parents about the way children with ADHD may have difficulty with:

Language skills

They may be disorganised in the way they tell a story, fail to recognise conversational cues, switch topics and not be able to predict the consequences of their words.

Social skills

They may have poor leisure and play skills, poor listening skills, lack of selective attention, lose eye contact, do inappropriate things at inappropriate times and have difficulty with understanding another person's point of view (so will have difficulty judging what communications will please, offend or engender conflict).

Behaviour problems

They may act thoughtlessly, have poor impulse control, have difficulty staying on task, have poor strategies for completion of tasks, seek immediate gratification and be unable to adapt their behaviour. They have difficulty planning and carrying out plans.

Visual and motor problems

They may have difficulty with motor co-ordination, be clumsy, have poor motor planning, visual motor difficulties and difficulties with visual motor integration (for example, copying, visual tracking, doing fine motor tasks, differentiating between figure and ground and recognising positions in space). Thus they may have difficulty in following trajectories and in catching.

Distractability

They may have difficulty tuning out to visual and auditory distractions.

Memory

They may have poor memory, and poor memory for rules.

Self-esteem

The-self esteem of children with ADHD is affected because of difficulties listed above.

Describe the overall group goals for the children's group as follows:

1. To help the children practise and enhance skills where there are difficulties as described.
2. To help the children feel good about themselves.
3. To help the children take responsibility for the problems they have as a result of ADHD.

10.20am Group activity for parents. Invite parents to draw a picture of their children's Attention Deficit Hyperactivity Disorder.

Process the drawings by asking, 'What would you like to do with your picture?', 'Who owns it?', 'How does it affect others?', 'Who is responsible for it?' and facilitate the sharing of experiences.

10.40am Outline the programme content and explain that the activities are designed to address:

- staying on task
- dealing with distractions
- impulse control
- memory tasks (visual and auditory)
- social and play skills
- language skills
- making transitions from one activity to another
- visual perceptual activities (to deal with tracking, focusing, visual-motor integration and/or planning and figure ground problems)
- motor activities (fine motor, position in space, and motor co-ordination activities)

Tell the parents that the group is designed to enable their children to learn new skills and to enable them to begin to take responsibility for their ADHD. Explain that a token system will be used to reinforce the behaviours stated in the daily goals.

10.50am Morning tea.

11.00am Close

Materials needed for this session

Drawing paper, coloured felt pens, photocopies of information to be distributed to parents and refreshments.

Day two – joining

Goals

To provide an opportunity for the children to meet each other and understand the purpose of the group.

172

The programme

10.00am Use the joining activity 'hoops'. Then, while the children continue to sit in their hoops explain the purpose of the group and the token system. Give each child a clear plastic container in which to store earned tokens. Explain that at the end of each session, each child's total tally of tokens will be recorded on a poster. The tally will be cumulative as the programme continues.

10.10am Use the 'tape checklist' activity to invite the children to discuss whether any of the problems they experience are the same as those mentioned on the tape. Discuss the similarities and differences between children in the group. Discuss the problems that ADHD children might experience because of their difficulties.

Use a toy microphone to allow the children to take turns in sharing their information. Pass the microphone from one child to another to facilitate turn taking in conversation.

10.20am Play the game 'crows and cranes' to allow for physical movement.

10.25am Give out the work-sheet 'how do you relax'. Then have a whole group discussion on relaxation options, followed by fifteen minutes of progressive muscular relaxation.

10.45am Use the motor activity 'Simon says' to provide an opportunity for the children to focus and pay attention.

10.50am Snack.

11.00am Close.

Materials needed for this session

Hoops, plastic containers for storing tokens, poster paper, audio-tape for the 'tape checklist' activity, a toy microphone, copies of the worksheet 'how to relax', and refreshments.

Day three – listening and following instructions

Goals

To help the children learn to focus, listen and follow instructions.

The programme

10.00am Check in using 'the weather chart'.

10.10am Ask the children to draw a self-portrait to allow them to focus on self, to discuss their personal attributes and become aware of their strengths and limitations.

10.20am Use the motor activity 'newspaper hockey' to provide an energy outlet.

10.30am Instruct the children in the use of selected pen and paper activities taken from puzzle books, such as 'join the dots', 'spot the difference' and 'find hidden objects'. These activities are to enhance listening skills and the ability to follow instructions.

10.40am Use the 'thinking skills' activity to help the children to learn to listen, problem solve and think logically. Continue with the 'word finding – verbal fluency' activity and the 'basic reasoning activity'.

10.50am Snack.

11.00am Close.

Materials needed for this session

A weather chart, drawing paper and coloured felt pens, old newspapers, pen and paper activities from puzzle books, and coloured hats.

Day 4 – turn taking and social interactions

Goals

To help the children learn to take turns and learn age appropriate ways of socially interacting.

The programme

10.00am Check in using the 'faces' work-sheet. Invite the children to draw faces to show how they are feeling.

10.10am Use the whole group activity 'roll the ball' to help the children understand turn taking behaviour.

10.20am In pairs use the game 'catch the sevens' to promote turn taking.

10.30am Play 'snap' to encourage turn taking.

10.40am Use the 'Partners' activity. This activity is played in pairs to encourage social skills involved in working with another child in a cooperative way.

10.50am Snack.

11.00am Close.

Materials needed for this session

Copies of the, 'what do people do with their faces' worksheet, poster paper, coloured felt pens, a tennis ball, a magazine picture with hidden 7's in it, Snap cards, assorted objects for the 'partners' activity, and refreshments.

Day 5 – transitions

Goal

To reduce the children's frustration levels when leaving tasks to start new ones.

The programme

10.00am Check in by using a set of miniature animals. Give the children the instruction, 'choose the animal which is just like you'. After the children have chosen their animals, process the activity, with each child talking about their perceptions of other children's animals as well as their own.

175

10.10am Use the 'paper chain' activity to help the children learn to cope with transitions from one activity to another.

10.20am Use the 'blow out the candles' activity to help the children learn to cope with transitions.

10.30am Use the 'the timer' activity to help the children learn to cope with transitions.

10.50am Snack.

11.00am Close.

Materials needed for this session

A selection of miniature animals, strips of colour paper for making paper chains, jigsaw puzzles, various materials for the 'timer activity' exercise, and refreshments.

Day 6 – visual memory, auditory memory and sequencing

Goal

To help the children improve visual and auditory memory and to raise their awareness of sequencing strategies.

The programme

10.00am Check in using the 'weather chart'.

10.10am Do the 'ring thing' activity in the whole group to help improve visual memory.

10.20am Do the 'fun box' activity in pairs to help the children experience co-operation and collaboration.

10.30am In the whole group, use the 'clothesline' activity to help the children attend and listen.

10.40am Do the 'pretty picture' activity with the whole group to improve visual memory.

10.50am Snack.

11.00am Close.

Materials needed for this session

A weather chart, five different rings, a variety of objects and a cardboard box for the 'fun box' activity, a clothes line, a green ribbon, items of dolls clothing, clothes pegs, a clothes basket, a collage, and refreshments.

Day 7 – organisation and planning

Goal

To help the children learn to plan more than one activity at a time.

The programme

10.00am Check in using the 'pick a pillow' activity.

10.10am Use the 'round robin' activity to help the children learn to cope with transitions.

10.20am Using the same activities as described above, place egg timers at each station. Get the children to estimate how long it would take them to complete each activity. As the children work, encourage them to use the timers to see how long it takes them to do what they have planned. This is to help the children learn to focus on a task and bring it to completion.

10.30am Use the 'television reporter' activity to encourage the children to talk about their activities and to improve their conversational skills.

10.50am Snack.

11.00am Close.

Materials needed for this session

Coloured cushions of various sizes, shapes, and designs, a variety of materials for the 'round robbing activity', the timers, a tape recorder and audio tape, and refreshments.

Day 8 – self esteem and saying 'goodbye'

Goals

To give the children an opportunity to feel good about themselves, to help the children understand their Attention Deficit Hyperactivity Disorder and to help the children say 'goodbye'.

The programme

10.00am Check in: ask the children to choose a miniature animal to represent themselves. Then ask them to talk to the group about the animals they selected.

10.10am Do the 'all about me' work-sheet. Emphasise that ADHD is only a part of a child and that there are many other things that make a child special.

10.20am Play 'crows and cranes'. This is a motor activity to give the children the opportunity to have some fun.

10.30am Ask the children to work in pairs and use toy telephones (or old telephones) to call their partners. They are to introduce themselves and ask their partners for help with one thing that they find difficult. For example, a child might say, 'Hello, I'm Jane. Sometimes I have difficulty with. . . . Could you help me?' This is to give the children confidence in their ability to find solutions.

10.40am Do the work-sheet 'I can do anything' (Geldard and Geldard, 1997). This is a work-sheet which stimulates discussion about which parts of self the children feel most comfortable in expressing at different times and in different situations. For example, a child may feel powerful and strong when with his or her peers yet submissive with his or her parents. When using this work-sheet it is important to promote the idea that it is okay to behave differently in different circumstances, and to explore the need to be adaptive and considerate of others.

10.50am Snack.

11.00am Close.

Materials needed for this session

A selection of miniature animals, copies of the 'all about me' worksheet, pencils or pens, toy telephones, copies of the 'I can do anything' worksheet, and refreshments.

12 Self-esteem programme

This chapter describes a programme for children who have low self-esteem. The topics for the programme are based on assumptions that children who have low self-esteem may have the following problems:

- Difficulty discovering their positive attributes
- Difficulty accepting their limitations
- Unrealistic expectations of self
- Maladaptive behaviours that have been developed to hide unattractive parts of self
- Difficulty deciding on values, beliefs and attitudes
- Difficulty with creativity
- Behaviours that are frightened, anxious and ambivalent
- Difficulty making and reaching goals
- Difficulty in accepting differences within themselves
- Irrational beliefs
- An inability to make use of cognitive or other healing strategies to help them feel better
- Feelings of disempowerment, helplessness and victimisation
- Feelings of incompetence
- Poor social skills (see Chapter 9)

Akin *et al.* (1990) consider that self-esteem is the emotional result of an ever-changing collection of accurate and/or inaccurate assessments one continually makes of oneself. These assessments are based on the way one views oneself (self-image) and thinks about oneself (self-concept) relative to numerous personal characteristics such as physical appearance, personality traits, status in various groups and the like. It is therefore advisable for any self-esteem programme for children to include elements which address both self-image and self-concept.

THE PROGRAMME

The programme is intended for children aged seven to nine years. It is of one-and-a-half hours duration each week, for a total of eight weeks. Children joining the programme need to be assessed, as described in Chapter 6, prior to being accepted to join the group.

The programme is suitable for either continuous evaluation or pre- and post-test evaluation. Using continuous evaluation, outcomes may be evaluated according to the achievement of session goals as listed at the beginning of the programme for each session. When using pre- and post-test evaluation, suitable assessment instruments are the Piers–Harris Children's Self Concept Scale (Piers and Harris, 1984) and the Coopersmith Self Esteem Inventories (Coopersmith, 1981).

The programme assumes that the group will be primarily run as a counselling and personal growth group, with an emphasis on the use of experiential and post-modern approaches. A pro-active leadership style is recommended.

The programme stresses weekly themes such as prehistoric land and outer space to set scenes where the children can discover positive attributes in themselves within a make-believe setting. This provides an opportunity for the children to build new stories about themselves which they previously may not have considered. The 'joining' and 'goodbye' sessions involve both parents and children, so that parents are able to witness and authenticate the children's stories about themselves. The remaining sessions involve the children without their parents. The weekly programme is:

1. Joining
2. Prehistoric land
3. Outer space
4. Amazon jungle
5. Desert island
6. Wonderland
7. Fantasy world
8. Saying 'Goodbye'

Week I – joining (for parents and children)

Goals

To help the children to join the group with the support of their parents and to give parents experience of the group process to be used.

The programme

2.00pm Use the joining activity 'balloon game'.

2.15pm Invite the group (both parents and children) to discuss the question 'what is self-esteem?' Write ideas about self-esteem on poster paper. Include the following ideas: knowing who you are, knowing what you can and cannot do, feeling good about yourself, being a good friend to yourself and identifying strengths and limitations.

Next, invite the group to discuss the factors that contribute to self-esteem. Write suggestions on poster paper. Include the following ideas: communicating and listening, receiving positive messages, feeling different, knowing it is okay to be different, getting on with other people, learning about others, letting other people get to know you, respecting others, having faith in each other, accepting each other and encouraging self-confidence.

2.35pm Use the 'If I was a . . .' work-sheet to help the children to imagine themselves as something different (for example, a racing car), and then to identify the features they would admire about themselves if they were this thing. This can be done in child–child, parent–parent, or child–parent pairs.

2.40pm Use the 'My Mum/Dad say things like . . .' work-sheet. This will be done in parent–child pairs, where the children are paired with their own parents. This is to help the parents and children identify how well they know each other.

2.45pm Snack

3.00pm Describe session programmes for the following weeks. Explain that each week the activities will have as their theme a journey through a different land. Also explain that each week group members will be given tokens to encourage participation, to reward children who help others out, as rewards for cooperative and caring behaviour, and whenever children identify their particular strengths or limitations.

Explain that during each weekly session there will be tasks and activities which will provide opportunities for the following:

- Cooperation (involving sharing, compromising and negotiating)
- Caring for others
- Verbal and non-verbal communication
- Success
- Problem solving (involving selecting the best options)
- Having fun
- Issues concerned with contact and boundaries
- Leadership
- Risk-taking, and consequences

Explain that during the activities in the programme there will be challenges involving varying degrees of difficulty for the children. Challenges will include decision-making, leadership problems, accepting limited choices and options and the development of personal strategies and resources.

3.10pm The 'Hotspots' activity will be used to metaphorically illustrate some of the obstacles and challenges which will be presented during the coming weeks, and the skills required to deal with these.

3.20pm Working in small groups, ask parents and children to make a collage using pictures from magazines. Then invite each group to make up a story based on their collage. This will be done by someone in the group making a statement about the picture to begin the story. Then other people/ children will each add a statement to progressively build on the story. Do the activity in groups of four, each consisting of two children and two parents. Process the activity in terms of collaborative storytelling and affirm each participant's contribution.

3.30pm Close.

Materials needed for this session

Sticky labels, coloured felt pens, balloons, a tape or CD player to play music, poster paper, copies of the 'If I was a . . .' work-sheet, copies of the 'my Mum/Dad say things like . . .' work-sheet, tokens, paper plates, a variety of magazines containing pictures, and refreshments.

Week 2 – prehistoric land

Goals

To help the children accept differences within themselves, between themselves and others, and to help them discover their expectations of themselves and accept their limitations.

The programme

2.00pm Check in using the 'weather chart' activity and the 'joining' activity.

2.15pm Decide on group rules and consequences. Write these on poster paper and stick them to the wall.

2.30pm Make a poster of a thermometer as described in the 'thermometer' activity and explain how this will be used to record accumulated tokens.

2.35pm Tell the group, 'Today you are going on a journey to hunt dinosaurs. You will need to choose a team-leader and follow a trail through a swamp. You will need to help each other through. You will know when you are getting close to the dinosaurs when you begin to find dinosaur eggs. You must prevent them from hatching. Finally you will need to research and identify the dinosaur that you are looking for. Then you will split into two groups to find the dinosaur. The team-leaders will be responsible for organising the groups through each stage of the hunt.' Then use the following exercises to help the children imagine they are going on the journey.

2.40pm Use the 'polarities' work-sheet. After completing this, process it with regard to leadership qualities, and similarities and differences between group members.

Ask the children to form two groups. In each group, ask the children to choose a leader by putting their names on pieces of paper in a hat or box and then picking out a name.

2.45pm Tell the children that one part of the room is a swamp. It can be marked off with masking tape or in some other way. Then explain how to play the 'back seat driver' game. Children who have been chosen as leaders will then be responsible for organising their teams (that is, deciding who goes first, etc.) so that they can get across the swamp. On completion, this activity will be processed in terms of accepting and giving instructions, cooperating, encouraging and supporting others.

2.55pm Snack.

3.10pm Use the 'pass the trash' activity. This is a game in which the children are encouraged to imagine they have discovered a dinosaur nest with eggs in it. The object is for one team to get the dinosaur eggs into the nest (which is the rubbish bin). This game is just for fun.

3.20pm Use the 'find the dinosaur' activity to identify and find the dinosaur. Process this activity by highlighting resourcefulness and strengths with regard to the demands of particular situations or tasks.

3.30pm Close.

Materials needed for this session

A weather chart, cushions, poster paper, coloured felt pens, copies of the 'polarities' work-sheet, small pieces of paper, a hat or box, masking tape, blindfolds, a large rubbish bin, old newspapers, two dinosaurs jigsaw puzzle's, tokens, and refreshments.

Week three – outer space

Goals

To encourage the children to express themselves in ways which will enable others to understand their needs and desires.

The programme

2.00pm As a check-in activity, invite the children to describe themselves as aliens and explain how they feel as aliens. They may then compare these feelings with how they feel in everyday life.

2.05pm Describe an imaginary planet in the universe. Divide the children into two groups. One group of children will pretend to

185

be astronauts from a space-ship, and the other group will pretend to be aliens. Tell the children 'The astronauts have landed on a planet inhabited by aliens. Their goal is to get to know the aliens because the aliens have materials which will enable them to fix their space-ship so that they can return to earth. In the end some aliens will return with the astronauts in the space-ship to earth.'

2.10pm Tell children that the astronauts and aliens are going to meet each other on the planet. Encourage the astronauts to rehearse some non-verbal behaviours which will introduce them to the alien group and help them to befriend the alien group. Simultaneously, encourage the aliens to rehearse their responses to the group of foreign astronauts who will land on their planet. Next, encourage the children to mime their first encounters with each other. Process the mime in terms of discovering and interpreting feelings and thoughts without the use of words. Invite the children to talk about whether the non-verbal greetings were friendly or unfriendly, welcoming, worrying or confusing, etc. Give affirmations with regard to the children's performances.

2.30pm Use the 'space encounter' activity. Process this in terms of self-disclosure, risk-taking, etc.

2.40pm Snack.

2.55pm Tell the children to work in pairs, with each pair consisting of one child from the alien group and one child from the astronauts' group. Invite children in each pair to get to know each other by using the 'I think, I feel, I want' activity. Process this with regard to learning new things about someone else and discovering things about themselves.

3.10pm Use the 'fix my space-ship' activity with the children working in their respective groups of aliens and astronauts. Ask the aliens to remember and then decide what objects they can give the astronauts. Ask the astronauts to remember the objects they need to fix their space-ship.

3.20pm Use the 'take me back' activity. Then adapt the 'crows and cranes' game so the two teams are called 'Martians' (the alien group) and 'Marstronauts' (the astronaut group). If the aliens are caught they become part of the space team and are taken back to earth.

3.30pm Close.

Materials needed for this session

A variety of objects for the 'fix my spaceship' activity, copies of the 'coded messages' work-sheet, writing paper and pens, tokens, and refreshments.

Week four – Amazon jungle

Goal

To help the children begin to explore their values, beliefs and attitudes.

The programme

2.00pm Check in using the 'choose an animal just like me' activity.

2.10pm Explain to the group that they are journeying into a jungle. In the jungle they will come across people who live there and who like to barter or swap their possessions. They may also come across other people who engage in very bad behaviour. In the jungle there are frogs and these are very important to the people who live in the jungle. If, on the journey, they take frogs with them the jungle dwellers will be pleased with them. In the jungle they will need to cross a river and to be aware that there are some very powerful animals around.

2.15pm Divide the group into two small groups. One group is the city dwellers and the other group is the people who live in the jungle. (Before the group starts, the leaders need to find pictures of items that might be useful for people who live in the city and pictures of items that might be useful for people who live in the jungle). Give each group some pictures of city objects and some pictures of jungle objects. The children are to imagine that these pictures are the objects. The groups will then be instructed to barter with members of the opposite group to gain objects which are going to be of most use to them, taking into account where they live. However, the jungle dwellers need to keep some objects that will be useful for living in the city, so that when they visit the city they have some objects which will be of use to them. Likewise, the city dwellers need to keep some objects that will allow them to

187

live in the jungle comfortably until they return to the city. The activity focuses on negotiating, collaborating and cooperating.

2.30pm In the whole group, the children will be invited to suggest a list of negative behaviours that are common to some bad people who live in this jungle. For example:

- Stealing fishing nets
- Lying about the stealing
- Boasting about the elephant hunt
- Bullying the smaller men in the village
- Back chatting the medicine man
- Not attending a meeting in preparation for the hunt
- Avoiding building the camp fire when directed to by the chief

Ask each child to rank the items starting with the most reprehensible act and proceeding to the least objectionable act. Then invite the children to discuss each item and as a group make a decision about which is the most negative behaviour. Processing will involve exploring differences in values, beliefs and attitudes.

2.45pm Snack

3.00pm Use the 'make a frog' work-sheet to make frogs which can be exchanged to show goodwill between the jungle and city dwellers. This is an activity that can be done in pairs so that an opportunity to give to others can be encouraged. Each pair will include a child from the city dwellers and a child from the jungle dwellers. The activity can be processed in terms of showing goodwill. Also, this may encourage recognition that giving can include giving of self, time, kindness, etc. and is not limited just to the giving of material possessions.

3.20pm Use the 'stepping stones' activity as a relay game to get across an imaginary river. After the game, process it in terms of collaboration, competition, support, etc.

3.30pm Close.

Materials needed for this session

A variety of miniature animals, a variety of pictures of items that might be useful for people who live in the city and of items that might be useful for people who live in the jungle, poster paper, felt pens, copies of the 'make a frog' work-sheet, sheets of paper for the 'stepping stones' activity, tokens, and refreshments.

Week five – desert island

Goals

To help the children experience their creativity and learn how this may be used as a strategy to help them feel better.

The programme

2.00pm Check in using the 'what do people do with their faces?' work-sheet.

2.10pm Seat the children in a circle while the rest of the session's activities are described. Divide the group into two teams. Give each child a 'Chart your course' work-sheet, a code interpreter (the top half of the 'codes and coded messages' work-sheet) and four sealed envelopes. Each envelope is to contain one coded message cut out of the 'codes and coded messages' work-sheet. The messages in code need to be decoded by the children so they gain information about where to go next on the treasure map given on the 'chart your course' work-sheet. The children are each to open one envelope at a time, decode the message, follow the decoded instruction to go to a particular station and complete the activity at the relevant station before opening the next envelope.

The leader needs to locate four stations around the room and one 'X marks the spot' place, as indicated on the 'chart your course' work-sheet. Located at each station will be an activity to be performed and completed by each child.

Station one is where children will individually complete the work-sheet 'fantasy friend'. Encourage the children to be as creative as they wish.

Station two will involve an activity, carried out individually, using craft materials (dolly pegs, pipe cleaners, cotton wool, glitter, etc.) to make a village dweller.

Station three will involve the children finding a partner and each pair completing the 'body image' activity.

Station four will involve the activity 'stepping stones'.

Finally, after all four messages have been decoded and the tasks completed, the child moves to 'X marks the spot' and makes a clay sculpture of what he or she believes is the hidden treasure.

Begin by taking the group to the start, as indicated by the star on the map. Ask the whole group to invent a story describing how they got to the island. The story needs to include answers to questions which start with 'who', 'what', 'when', 'where', 'why' and 'how'. Write the story on a large piece of cardboard.

Next, the children move to each location by choosing one envelope at a time, opening it, and following the directions in it. Each child must have evidence of having been in each station to take back to his or her team at the end of the process. Each team will earn tokens, to be distributed equally among members, when every member has completed the island course.

This session is not divided into time slots but allows the children to leisurely pass through each station at their own pace. The activity is followed by a snack and processing of the experience. Children who have completed all tasks may ask other children if they would like help and, if so, assist them in their tasks.

3.15pm Process the activity in terms of issues of cooperative participation, independent activity and creativity.

3.30pm Close

Materials needed for this session

Copies of the 'what do people do with their faces?' work-sheet, the 'chart your course' work-sheet, the 'codes and coded messages' work-sheet, and the 'fantasy friend' work-sheet, four envelopes containing coded messages, pencils or pens, craft materials, large sheets of poster paper, coloured felt pens, sheets of paper to be used as stepping stones, tokens, and refreshments.

Week six – Wonderland

Goals

To help the children experience feelings of competence and learn goal-directed behaviour.

The programme

2.00pm Check in using the activity 'pick a pillow'.

2.10pm Place a large version of the 'game board' work-sheet, drawn on large sheets of poster paper, on the floor. Ask the children to sit in a circle around it and explain its use. Invite the children to work in pairs with each pair being given one dice. Tell them that when they land on a space they must read and follow the instructions in that space before they can throw their dice again to move around the board to progress towards the finish.

There are no time segments for this session. The children must play the game several times until they have completed all the tasks which they have not completed in previous games. When children have completed their journey around the game board they can break for a snack. When all children have completed the game board journey, processing of the session's activities can begin.

The children may need assistance from the group leaders to complete this activity.

3.15pm Processing will be in terms of accomplishing tasks, following instructions, success in meeting goals, encouragement, support, working independently and helping and receiving help.

3.30pm Close

Materials needed for this session

A variety of coloured cushions of various sizes, shapes, and designs, a large version of the 'game board' work-sheet, tokens, and refreshments.

Week seven – fantasy world

Goals

To provide the children with an opportunity to work closely and cooperatively with others and to help minimise anxious, frightened or ambivalent behaviours.

The programme

2.00pm Check in using the 'draw a feeling' activity. Invite the children to draw a line, shape or picture to describe how they are feeling at the present moment.

2.10pm Explain the following:

- The activities today will focus around a journey into fantasy world
- The group will be divided into four small working groups and begin a journey into fantasy land by making a castle
- The small groups will then search for the castle in a magic forest
- They will need to complete a maze which will show them how to get to the castle, and will then have to hide from the creatures in the magic forest
- They will make a booklet of the different creatures in the forest (which keep changing)
- They will complete a story about their visit to the magic forest

Having explained the above, ask the children to work in small groups. Using expanded polystyrene boxes (subject to safety considerations), packing material, construction and other craft materials, each group is to make a magic castle. The activity will then be processed in terms of collaboration, cooperation, sharing, turn taking, etc.

2.35pm Next, the children will be invited to complete the 'demon maze' work-sheet in order to find their way to the castle.

2.45pm Snack.

3.00pm Play the game 'sardines'. Incorporate the game into the theme by suggesting the children have to find a safe spot to hide for the night in the magic forest. Process this activity in terms of hiding from, or dealing with, fears and anxieties, and the usefulness of support.

3.10pm Give each child 'forest creatures' work-sheet, which they can cut out and staple together to form a booklet containing pictures of various creatures and monsters they might meet in the magic forest. Each page is then cut along the dotted lines so that the appearances of the creatures can be altered by turning half pages. Process with regard to unpredictable change being a source of anxiety and the discovery of inner resources for coping.

3.20pm Ask the children, working in pairs, to complete the blanks in the 'magic forest' work-sheet. Process this in terms of how the story reflects the children's own responses in life and how they might change their responses.

3.30pm Close.

Materials needed for this session

Drawing paper, coloured felt pens, expanded polystyrene boxes (subject to safety considerations), packing materials, construction and other craft materials, copies of the 'demon maze', 'forest creatures' and 'magic forest' work-sheets, a stapler, tokens, and refreshments.

Week eight – saying 'goodbye' (for parents and children)

Goals

To experience feelings of success, control, support and the companionship with others.

The programme (for parents and children)

2.00pm Check in using the 'weather chart'.

2.10pm Play the game 'human tunnel ball' with parents competing against children.

2.20pm Divide the group into two teams to use the 'sticker' activity. Process this activity in terms of recognising individual differences and noticing the positive attributes of others.

2.30pm Snack.

2.45pm Invite the children to spend their tokens they have earned during the programme as described in the first session. Each parent will have been invited to bring in one, or a few, small novelty items of low value. Display these items, with prices marked in tokens, so the children can buy them with tokens.

3.00pm Snack

3.15pm   Play 'crows and cranes'.

3.20pm   Ask each child to choose a symbol to represent how they feel about having been in the group during the eight weeks period. Ask parents to choose symbols to represent what they have noticed about their children since the group started.

3.30pm   Close.

Materials needed for this session

A weather chart, sticky labels containing messages for the 'sticker' activity, novelty items for the children to buy with tokens, a box of small items to be used as symbols, tokens, and refreshments.

13 Social skills programme

There has been a recent upsurge in interest in improving the social skills of children who present with chronic and marked social relationship behaviours that are unacceptable to others and personally unsatisfying. As might be expected, it is difficult to improve social skills by working with children individually because social skills involve the use of interactional behaviours. However, group programmes such as the one described in this chapter can be useful in helping children improve their social skills.

There are a number of important reasons for promoting social skills. Where children are unable to build social relationships with others they are likely to experience anxiety in social situations and they may withdraw. Children with poor social skills may be rejected by their peers and have an increased risk of emotional and behavioural difficulties. Research findings suggest a strong relationship between social competence in childhood and social, academic and psychological functioning (O'Rourke and Worzbyt, 1996). We also know that children with poor social skills are unable to initiate and maintain interaction with others in a positive manner. As a consequence they are likely to be ignored, or suffer rejection. They may be actively disliked, blamed and maltreated by other children. Consequently they are often depressed and unhappy children. On the other hand children with adaptive social skills are likely to be popular, have friends and be happier. There is therefore a strong case for addressing social skills deficits in children. Additionally, an emphasis on teaching social skills to children has grown in recent years because of the importance of socially effective behaviour on subsequent development (Rose and Edleson, 1987).

The topics for this programme are based on assumptions that children who have difficulty with social skills have the following problems (Levine *et al.*, 1987):

- Difficulty engaging in cooperative play
- Difficulty with social conversation

- Difficulty terminating interactions with others, so they may do so abruptly
- Difficulty timing and staging friendships (for example, they may take liberties too early in relationships, or treat new friendships as if they were of long standing)
- Difficulty giving positive responses when others initiate contact
- Difficulty contributing, in a relevant way, to group conversation
- Difficulty identifying and expressing feelings
- Difficulty predicting the consequences of their behaviour
- Difficulty understanding social cues
- Difficulty accommodating the needs of others
- Difficulty adapting their behaviour to the needs of others
- Poor recuperative strategies
- Poor self-image and self-concept
- They tend to have very brief interactions with peers
- They may have more involvement in aggressive play than infriendly play
- They may use inappropriate verbal/non-verbal skills more frequently than most children
- They may make inappropriate and too frequent approaches to peers
- They may engage in more anti-social acts than most children
- They may tend to choose less socially acceptable behaviours

The difficulties listed above can be broadly conceptualised as fitting along three dimensions as described by Gajewski and Mayo (1989):

1. A *skill deficit*, which indicates that the child has not acquired the necessary social skill. For example, a child may be unable to appropriately accept a compliment because the child has never been taught to say 'thankyou'.
2. A *performance deficit*, where the child has the skill, but doesn't perform it, because of anxiety, low motivation or feelings of incompetence.
3. A *self-control deficit*, where the child lacks adequate behaviours to control impulsive, disruptive or aggressive social behaviour. In this case, the child's lack of self-control interferes with the performance of learnt skills.

THE PROGRAMME

Each session of this programme includes strategies to address deficits along the three dimensions of skills deficits, performance deficits and self-control deficits, as described by Gajewski and Mayo (1989). The programme makes use of cooperative learning techniques because these have been shown to encourage group interaction and promote interdependence. This is helpful to children with low self-esteem because of the difficulty they have interacting cooperatively with others. Cooperative learning makes use of face-to-face interactions and holds each child accountable for learning material which can provide support and assistance to other children in the group. In this programme emphasis is placed on helping the children to understand social skill concepts through verbal instruction, modelling and rehearsal of skills as suggested by King and Kirschenbaum (1992).

It is often assumed that the use of social skills within a group setting will automatically generalise to other settings. However, research regarding this assumption suggests that teaching social skills in a group does not necessarily result in generalisation of skills. For generalisation, the children need to be provided with motivating influences which will encourage use of the skills (Adelman and Taylor, 1982). Use of rewards and consequences is therefore an integral part of this group programme. King and Kirschenbaum (1992) suggest that generalization may be enhanced through the use of homework assignments for the child together with providing the parents with information concerning the programme which will enable them to be supportive of the child's learning of new skills.

Each session follows a consistent formula, as it:

- Introduces a specific social skill
- Emphasises the importance of self-regulated learning by encouraging the children to use self-talk. This is useful because it encourages children to manage both their cognitive abilities and motivational level (Harris, 1984)
- Includes the modelling of social skills and self-talk to self-regulate behaviour
- Includes role-plays to practise the use of social skills
- Processes (encourages discussion of) the children's experiences during structured and unstructured activities

The programme runs for one-and-a-half hours each week for ten weeks, and is suitable for children aged nine to twelve years. Children joining the programme need to be assessed, as described in Chapter 6, prior to being accepted to join the group. The programme is suitable for pre- and post-test evaluation with outcomes being evaluated according to the achievement of listed session goals. The programme assumes that the group will be primarily run as a psycho-educational and counselling group using a cognitive–behavioural approach. A pro-active, tending towards authoritarian, leadership style will suit this programme. The weekly programme is:

1. Parent information session.
2. Getting to know you.
3. Expressing feelings.
4. Communicating.
5. Friendships.
6. Solving problems with friends.
7. Cooperating.
8. Chilling out.
9. Looking after yourself.
10. Goodbye.

Session one of the programme is for parents only, with the remaining sessions being for the children.

Week 1 – parent information session

Goals

To familiarise parents with the programme and enlist their cooperation.

The programme

Start with introductions. Discuss the problems experienced by children with poor social skills as listed in the assumptions. Describe the programme to the parents, discuss the homework activities the children will be required to do, and stress the importance of parental support for these activities. End the session with afternoon tea to give parents an opportunity to interact informally and ask questions.

Materials needed for this session

Handout material for the parents describing the programme, and refreshments.

Week 2 – getting to know you

Goals

To meet other children in the group, decide on group rules and understand the purpose and format of the weekly group sessions.

The programme

2pm   Use the joining activity 'bingo cards'. Give each of the children a bingo card. The bingo cards are all identical with each card divided into nine squares. In each square is a description of a specific characteristic, behaviour or belief. Each child has to find a child whose answers match the words in one of the boxes. That child then introduces him or herself by name and signs in the appropriate box. The process continues until each child has signatures in three boxes in a row (horizontally, vertically or diagonally).

2.10pm   Process the bingo card activity in terms of getting to know others and sharing information about self. Invite the children to introduce other children, whose names they remember, to the whole group. Ask the children to wear sticky label name tags.

2.15pm   Invite the group to formulate and agree on group rules. Discuss the token system including the number of tokens to be given for specific behaviours that demonstrate observation of the group rules. Explain that tokens can be collected throughout the programme and be used in the final session to purchase small items from the token table.

2.20pm   Play the game 'crows and cranes' as a whole group activity to allow the children to move and raise their energy.

2.30pm   Use the 'Body image' game to help the children get to know each other.

2.40pm   Process the previous activity in terms of ease or difficulty in doing the task.

2.45pm   Snack.

3.00pm   Play the 'blind-fold' game.

3.10pm Process this activity in terms of advantages and disadvantages of non-verbal communication.

3.15pm Discuss the homework activity. During the week each child is to choose three people in their class and to find out some of the following information:

1. What are their favourite TV stars?
2. What did they do during the weekend?
3. Do they have brothers or sisters?
4. Do they have any pets?

3.20pm Describe the 'thermometer' activity as a way to record the cumulative number of tokens each child receives as the programme progresses. Explain that the children will receive tokens for attending, and participating in, the session and can add these to those they receive as rewards for appropriate behaviour.

Invite the children to colour in their individual 'thermometers' to record the total number of tokens they have each received in this session. Keep the thermometers so they can be used to show the acquisition of additional tokens over subsequent weeks.

3.30pm Close.

Materials needed for this session

Biango cards for the joining activity, sticky label name tags, large sheets of poster paper, coloured felt pens, blindfolds, tokens, and refreshments.

Week 3 – expressing feelings

Goals

To introduce, model, practise and process the skill of expressing feelings appropriately.

The programme

2.00pm Check in using the 'Pick a cushion' activity.

2.10pm Revise the rules, and the use of the thermometer chart for recording tokens. Discuss the experiences the children had when doing the homework exercise.

2.15pm Introduce today's topic which is 'identifying and expressing feelings'.

2.20pm Play the 'detective game'.

2.30pm Use the 'express your feelings' activity.

2.40pm Process these activities with regard to misunderstandings that can arise when interpreting mixed verbal and non-verbal messages.

2.45pm Snack.

3.00pm Invite the children to work individually on the work-sheet 'your body' (Geldard and Geldard, 1997). This explores the interpretation of non-verbal emotional feelings.

3.05pm Process the work-sheet using the four Ps, as described in the following, and discuss the importance of interpreting non-verbal feelings correctly.

1. Pause. Stop and think about what the problem, task or situation is. Then put this into a sentence.
2. Plan. Plan some of the things that you could do as solutions. List them no matter how silly they might be.
3. Perform. Choose one of the above and act on it. Your choice should be one which will be comfortable for you and will not infringe on the rights of other people.
4. Ponder. Now think about whether the solution you chose was a useful one or not. Evaluate it in terms of how you feel now, how the other person responded, and whether or not your goal was achieved.

3.10pm Model a role play with a child from the group which contains a mixed message as a result of differences between verbal and non-verbal communication. For example, as leader you might model use of a mixed message by expressing friendship using words 'Yes, I'd really love to be your friend' and 'Yeah, why don't we meet after school and go to the plaza', but with arms folded tightly across the chest and gazing into the distance.

3.15pm Invite the children to process the modelled role play using the four Ps.

3.20pm Working in pairs, give the children situations to role play using the, 'Expressing feelings – social skills role plays' activity.

3.25pm Process the previous activity using the four **Ps**.

3.30pm Give the children the homework task which is to practise one role play at home. Close.

Materials needed for this session

A variety of cushions of various colours, designs, and shapes, a thermometer chart, a piece of jewellery, copies of the work-sheet 'Your body', poster paper and felt pens to write up the 4 Ps, tokens, and refreshments.

Week 4 – topic communicating

Goals

To introduce, model, practise and process the skill of clear and appropriate ways to communicate

The programme

2.00pm Check in using the 'draw a feeling' activity, and then discuss the homework task set last week.

2.10pm Introduce the topic 'communicating'. Emphasise the need to listen, take turns, receive and give information.

2.15pm Use the game 'reporter'.

2.25pm Process this activity in terms of how messages become distorted and misunderstood, and the importance of listening and looking carefully.

2.30pm Use the work-sheet 'Questions' (Geldard and Geldard, 1997). This work-sheet shows children how, by asking questions beginning with 'What', 'Where', 'When', 'Why' and 'How' a story can develop. It demonstrates the way questions can be used to start conversations. Discussion of this work-sheet can include the problems associated with asking too many questions.

2.40pm Process the use of the work-sheet in terms of using questions in conversation to gain information.

2.45pm Snack.

3.00pm Introduce the idea of communicating in different ways. Talk about the way people can respond aggressively, passively or assertively.

3.10pm Describe a situation where friends begin to sing 'Happy birthday' to you in a public place, and you are embarrassed. Model an aggressive response, a passive response and an assertive response. Use the 'mouse and cheese poster' activity to illustrate successful and unsuccessful responses.

3.15pm Process this using the four **P**s.

3.20pm Use the 'communicating – social skills role plays' activity to provide each child with a role-play picked out of a hat. Divide them into pairs and ask them to act out their role-plays for their partners.

3.25pm Process the role-plays using the four **P**s.

3.30pm Give the children the homework task which is to practice one role play at home. Close.

Materials needed for this session

Drawing paper, coloured felt pens, a mouse and cheese poster with a cut out cardboard mouse attached by a piece of Velcro, pictures for 'the reporter' activity, copies of the work-sheet 'questions', tokens, and refreshments.

Week 5 – friendships

Goals

To introduce, model, practise and process the skill of initiating and maintaining friendships and resisting pressure in friendships.

The programme

2.00pm Check in using the 'choose a symbol' activity, and then discuss the homework task set last week.

2.10pm Introduce the topic 'friendships'. Discuss important elements of friendship including trust, similarities, loyalty and being able to say 'no' without hurting feelings, etc.

2.15pm Play the game 'hotspots'.

2.25pm Process this activity in terms of trust.

2.30pm Do the work-sheet activity 'Fantasy Friend'.

2.40pm Process this activity in terms of friends with similarities and differences to oneself.

2.45pm Snack.

3.00pm In the whole group get the children to brainstorm about the things they like (for example: watch quietly, share something, laugh at their jokes or match the conversation) and the things they do not like (for example: brag, interrupt, hang around or make unwanted physical contact) when other kids try to join them to make friends. Leaders need to be aware of differences between the way adults make contact and the way children make contact (for example: adults introduce themselves whereas children usually do not).

3.10pm Using a role-play, model the way to say 'no' to friends. Model the use of the 'Say "no" checklist' activity.

3.15pm Process the role-play using the four Ps.

3.20pm Ask a child to role play with a partner saying 'no' while the remaining group members use the 'Say "no" checklist' activity to evaluate the child's ability to say 'no' in a way which is okay for them and their partner.

3.25pm Process using the four Ps.

3.30pm The homework task is to practise saying 'no' appropriately at home. Close.

Materials needed for this session

A selection of objects suitable for use as symbols, paper plates, copies of the work-sheet 'fantasy friend', a poster of the 4 **P**s, tokens, and refreshments.

Week 6 – solving problems with friends

Goals

To introduce, model, practise and process the skill of problem solving.

The programme

2.00pm Check in using the 'weather chart' and then discuss the home-work task set last week.

2.10pm Reinforce the four Ps approach to solving problems.

2.15pm Play 'newspaper hockey'.

2.25pm Process this activity. See if the group can relate the four Ps approach to aspects of the activity.

2.30pm Use the work-sheet 'If then but . . .' (Geldard and Geldard, 1997): This is a work-sheet which invites children to explore the negative and positive consequences of particular behaviours.

2.40pm Process this activity in terms of the issue of loss which arises when making some decisions.

2.45pm Snack.

3.00pm Introduce the skill to be learnt. Describe three scenarios where a child responds to another omitting one of the Ps. The group is asked to identify, which 'P' has been missed out.

3.05pm Process this activity in terms of the value of using the four Ps process when problem solving.

3.10pm Model the use of the four Ps. Role play the following: Tom is playing a video game. His brother Bruce comes into the room, having finished his homework, and wants to play the next video game. Make this a humorous situation by using dress-up props and playing both roles. Other role-plays can be used in the same way to demonstrate the use of the four Ps.

3.15pm Process this activity using the four Ps.

3.20pm Use the, 'problem solving – social skills role plays' activity. Divide the group into two small groups with even numbers of children in each. Invite each child to choose a partner and to role-play a situation which is described on a piece of paper taken out of a hat. Give the rest of the group a check list of the four **P**s, and encourage them to tick the list whenever they notice the performer using one of the 'P' processes.

3.30pm The homework is to practise one role play at home. Close.

Materials needed for this session

A weather chart, old newspapers, copies of the work-sheet 'if, then, but . . .', a checklist for each child listing the **4 P**s, role play situations written on pieces of paper and put into a hat, tokens, and refreshments.

Week 7 – cooperating

Goals

To introduce, model, practise and process the skills required for cooperating.

The programme

2.00pm Check in using the 'what do people do with their faces' work-sheet. Then discuss the homework task set last week.

2.10pm Introduce the topic 'cooperating'. Include in the discussion the notion that cooperating might mean compromising. Describe and define compromise as occurring when each person gives up part of what they want in order to reach agreement. Talk about cooperating with one person, and cooperating with others in a large group. Explore the differences between these two situations.

2.15pm Use the 'find the dinosaur' activity.

2.25pm Process this activity with regard to cooperation.

2.30pm Do the 'cooperation collage'.

2.40pm Process this activity in terms of the need to agree and compromise.

2.45pm Snack.

3.00pm Introduce an exercise to teach the skills required for coopera-tion. Invite the children to brainstorm about how cooperation could occur in the following scenario: 'Imagine that you and your brother or sister share a room. Your mother and father have told you both go to your room and clean it up, because it is in a dreadful mess.' During the brainstorming write up the action words children use to explore the elements of cooperation (for example, planning, delegating, taking turns, sharing, identifying the goals, each person's beliefs about what they are prepared to do, the elements of time, speed and immediacy, etc). Discuss what each person might individually decide to give up.

3.05pm Process the activity in terms of planning, delegating, taking terms, sharing and identifying goals and beliefs.

3.10pm Model a situation where compromise occurs in a role play. Introduce the idea of trade offs, bartering, negotiating.

3.15pm Process this using the four Ps.

3.20pm Give the children a few examples of situations where they can role play making a compromise. Use a checklist from the previous brainstorming session to check the use of appro-priate strategies.

3.25pm Process this using the four Ps.

3.30pm The homework is to practise compromising in at least one situation at home. Close.

Materials needed for this session

Copies of the work-sheet 'what do people do with their faces', coloured felt pens, two dinosaur jigsaw puzzles, magazines containing pictures for the collage, poster paper, the 4 **P**s poster, tokens, and refreshments.

Week 8 – chilling out

Goals

To introduce, model, practise and process the skills required to take responsibility for and to manage one's own behaviour when relating to others.

207

The programme

2.00pm Use the check in activity 'pick a pillow'. Then discuss the homework task set last week.

2.10pm Introduce the topic 'self-management of behaviour'. In discussion of the topic, include the need for children to understand and recognise consequences, recover after making mistakes socially, present themselves in ways that are socially acceptable and to reinforce their own social behaviours in positive ways.

2.15pm Play the game 'spotto'.

2.25pm Process this activity with regard to holding back and showing restraint. Also explore how doing this feels.

2.30pm Use the 'feeling small' activity.

2.35pm Process this activity in terms of what the children might do, or say, when they experience feeling small and/or feeling left out. Explain that managing their behaviour in response to such experiences may be difficult. Explore options; for example, withdrawing, being pushy, becoming tearful, etc.

2.45pm Snack.

3.00pm Introduce the skill of self-management to the whole group. Ask what situations might occur where children need to manage their own emotional responses. For example, feeling left out, feeling embarrassed, feeling angry, feeling left alone, feeling threatened and feeling different from others. Discuss possible responses and/or practical solutions. Some of these might include self-talk, crying, giggling, screaming, breathing deeply and relaxing. Discuss the merits, and/or disadvantages of each of these solutions.

3.05pm Process the activity using the four Ps.

3.10pm Model a situation where a child may need to use self-management. Role play a situation where a child has been asked to answer a question in class but has not been listening. Model an inappropriate response for managing the situation and then model an appropriate response, where managing the behaviour is comfortable for the child.

3.15pm Process the activity using the four Ps.

3.20pm Use the 'self-management' role-play activity.

3.25pm Process the activity using the four **Ps**.

3.30pm The homework task is to practise one role-play at home. Close.

Materials needed for this session

A variety of cushions of differing colours, patterns, and shapes, clay or modelling dough, the 4 **Ps** poster, tokens, and refreshments.

Week 9 – looking after yourself

Goals

To introduce, model, practise and process the skills which can be helpful in affirming the child's own positive behaviours and accomplishments.

The programme

2.00pm Check in using the 'pass the ball' activity. Then discuss the homework task set last week.

2.10pm Introduce the topic 'looking after yourself'. Include issues around being and feeling safe, boundaries, checking perceptions of situations and recognising achievements, etc.

2.15pm Use the activity 'Personal boundaries' which involves the circle concept. This activity can be used to encourage the children to look after themselves emotionally and physically and to identify instances where they can either invite others into their personal space, or keep them out.

2.25pm Process the activity using the four **Ps**.

2.30pm Play the game 'sardines'.

2.40pm Process this in terms of personal space and boundaries.

2.45pm Snack.

3.00pm Introduce the skill of looking after yourself using the work-sheet 'Reward yourself' (Geldard and Geldard, 1997). This work-sheet allows the children to think about positive accom-

209

plishments at home and school, and to draw a picture or symbol to represent the accomplishment. Invite the children to think about their own positive accomplishments, to draw a picture or symbol of an accomplishment, and to discuss how achieving this made them feel.

3.05pm Process this activity focusing on feelings associated with achievement.

3.10pm Use a role-play to model an appropriate way to talk about having achieved success in achieving a goal.

3.15pm Process using the four **Ps**.

3.20pm Invite the children to think about situations where they have done well and to role-play how they would tell someone else about this (see the 'rewarding yourself – social skills role-play' activity)

3.25pm Process using the four **Ps**.

3.30pm The homework task is to practise one role play at home. Close.

Materials needed for this session

A large beach ball, a sheet of poster paper for each child with concentric circles drawn on it for the personal boundaries exercise, copies of the work-sheet 'reward yourself', coloured felt pens, the 4 **Ps** poster, tokens, and refreshments.

Week 10 – goodbye session

Goals

To review the whole programme and reinforce what has been learnt. To give the children an opportunity to spend the tokens they have earned.

The programme

2.00pm Check in by giving the children the instruction 'choose the animal which is most like you'. Then discuss the homework task set last week.

2.10pm Introduce the topic. The topic for today is revision and goodbye. Invite the children to complete evaluation sheets and tell them that today's session will involve many games where the skills from all the previous weeks will be practised. Tokens will be used to reinforce appropriate use of the skills during the activities.

2.15pm Use the 'man the lifeboat' activity.

2.25pm Process this in terms of the skills learnt during the previous weekly sessions.

2.30pm Work in pairs using the 'make a frog' work-sheet.

2.40pm Process this in terms of the skills learnt during the previous weekly sessions.

2.45pm Snack.

3.00pm Use the 'back seat drivers' game.

3.05pm Process this in terms of the skills learnt during the previous weekly sessions.

3.10pm Ask the children to count the number of tokens they have and invite them to spend their tokens at the token table. The token table will have various small novelty rewards, each labelled with a price expressed in tokens (the rewards can include low cost items such as bubble blowing sets, Barbie doll outfits, playing cards, pencil cases, erasers, super bouncing balls, etc.)

3.25pm Ask the children to hand in their evaluations and do the 'choose a symbol' activity. Invite them to choose a symbol to represent how they have felt about being in the group over the past 9 weeks.

3.30pm Close.

Materials needed for this session

A selection of miniature animals, evaluation sheets, masking tape or chalk, copies of the work-sheet 'make a frog', blindfolds, tokens, novelty rewards to be purchased with tokens, a variety of objects to be used as symbols, and refreshments.

Appendix A: Activities and games

The activities, games and video tapes listed in this appendix are ones which have been found suitable for use in group work with children. They are included in the group programmes for specific target groups given in Chapters 10 to 13. Some of the games and activities require energy and physical skills, so leaders need to be aware of, and attend to, issues of safety at all times.

Abuse continuum: Stick a long sheet of poster paper on a wall with a scale from 1 to 10 drawn along its length. Label 1 as representing not being abusive and 10 as representing the most abusive act that could ever happen. Give each child several sheets of A4 paper. Invite them to write words that describe abusive actions or activities on their A4 sheets of paper, and then stick these onto the poster paper. In doing this, they must judge where their sheets of paper should be placed along the scale to indicate the severity of the abuse. Discuss with the whole group the concept that 'abuse is not okay' regardless of severity.

Back seat drivers: Blindfold two children and ask them to form a seat by grasping each other's wrists. Ask another child to sit on the seat and become a driver. Without speaking, the driver's task is to lead the blindfolded pair around obstacles. This game can be played as a group effort competing against the clock, or as a relay.

Balloon game: Ask each child to:

1. Write his or her name on a sticky label which still has the backing on it.
2. Without removing the backing fold the label and insert it into a balloon.
3. Blow up the balloon and tie it up.

Next, invite the children to form a large group. Tell them you will play some music and that while the music is playing they are to hit the balloons so they move around the room. While the music is playing the balloons must be kept in the air and not hit the floor. When the music stops, tell the children to pick up the balloon nearest them and burst it (some children may need some help with this). When the balloons are burst, each child is to take the name tag from their balloon and search for the child whose name tag they have. When they find the child, they introduce themselves and share one thing about themselves that they don't mind the other child knowing (for example, their favourite food). Once all the children have their own name tags, they are invited to re-join the big group. Then they each introduce to the whole group the child who gave them their name tag. If they can remember the information shared by that child they may also pass this information on to the whole group.

Basic reasoning: To help improve basic reasoning the leader asks questions such as 'do you feel happier when you lose a game or when you win?', 'how many eggs could you hold at one time?', 'you can drink water. What else can you do with it?', 'can you kick with your hands?', etc.

Bingo cards: Each child is given a card divided into nine squares of three rows and three columns. In each square is one of the following statements: 'Find someone wearing joggers', 'Find someone who uses the same toothpaste as you', 'Find someone who wears glasses', 'Find someone who is eight years old', 'Find someone who has their hair in a pony tail', 'Find someone who has a birthday in May', 'Find someone who likes cauliflower', 'Find someone who is the youngest child in the family' and 'Find someone who has a pet'. The children are invited to mingle with each other and ask questions to find children who fit descriptions given on the card. When a child finds another child who fits a description, that other child initials the relevant square on the first child's card. A child is not allowed to initial more than one square on any other child's card. The goal is to score a bingo by having initials in three squares in the same horizontal or vertical row, or diagonal. When a child achieves this, he or she can shout, 'bingo!' The game may continue until one of the children has completed all nine squares.

Blindfold game: The children form pairs and one of each pair is blindfolded. Pairs stand together at one end of the room. Obstacles are placed in the room on the floor. In each pair, the blindfolded child is to be physically led by their partner safely across the room without talking. Each pair then exchanges the blindfold and repeats the process. Finally, the game is processed with regard to the use of non-verbal information.

Blow out the candles: Place a number of jigsaw puzzles around a large table (more puzzles than children). Each child begins a puzzle and when it is complete signals that they are moving to another puzzle by blowing out pretend birthday candles, using the five fingers on each hand as the pretend candles. Children can complete the circuit as many times as they wish as long as they blow out the pretend candles each time they move to a new puzzle. This activity is useful in helping children cope with transitions from one activity to another.

Body image game: The children form pairs. One partner stands with his or her back against a sheet of paper on the wall while the other draws around his/her body. They change places and use another sheet of paper to repeat the process. Each child then fills in the physical details for their partner, such as facial features, clothes, etc.

Catch the sevens: On any magazine picture, mark in the number seven in several hidden positions on the page. Each child takes turns to find a seven and draw a circle around it. The concept of missing a turn can be introduced if a child is unable to locate a number seven and says, 'I'll miss my turn'.

Choose a symbol: This is a check-in activity. Each child selects an object from a box of objects (symbols) to describe how he or she feels. They share this with the rest of the group. For example, a child.may choose a tennis ball and describe how the object is round, bouncy, rolls away and has fun. Thus, the child can express how he or she feels.

Choose an animal to show how I feel: Children choose an animal from a pile of assorted miniature animals to represent how they are feeling. The choice of animal is then processed in the group. Other children may be invited to try to guess how each child may be feeling by looking at the animal chosen.

Clothesline: This is a good activity for improving visual memory. String up a nylon line to make a clothesline that is within the children's reach. Tie a green ribbon on the left end of the line to signal the start. Tell a story about someone hanging out laundry, and include items of doll's clothing in the story. As you mention each item, hang it on the line. Next, explain that the clothes are now dry, take them down and put them into the clothes basket. Once the items have been placed in the basket, ask the children to hand you the items in the order they were hanging on the line.

Communicating – social skill role plays: The children are encouraged to role play the following scenarios:

1. You've made plans with two friends. While you are getting ready another friend comes along and asks if she can join you. You don't want to include her. What do you say?
2. Your teacher gave you a very low mark on your report. You believe that you deserved better. How would you approach the situation?
3. You're in the library and need to concentrate on a difficult task. The students next to you are talking and chewing gum. How will you respond?
4. A very close friend constantly interrupts you while you are speaking. What will you do?
5. A casual acquaintance teases you in a joking way. This is beginning to annoy you. What will you do?

Cooperation collage: The children are divided into groups of three and instructed to make a collage around a particular topic. While making the collage, each group is provided with only one pair of scissors, one glue stick and two magazines. The limited resources and need to agree about where to place pictures on the page facilitate the exploration of cooperative behaviour.

Copycat: The children sit in a circle, except for one, who stands outside the circle. One child in the circle leads an action such as clapping, hitting knees, winking, etc., and is responsible for changing this action at will. The person outside the circle who has been brought from another room tries to guess who is the leader. When the leader is identified, the leader exchanges places with the person who is outside the circle and leaves the room. A new leader is selected before the game continues.

Crown Prince: Video tape produced by Kids Rights, 10100 Park Cedar Drive, Charlotte, NC 28210 USA.

Crows and cranes: The group divides into two equal teams. One team is called 'the crows' and the other 'the cranes'. The teams line up facing each other and about two metres apart. The group leader calls out either 'Crows' or 'Cranes'. When the leader calls 'crows', the crows chase the cranes and try to capture them by touching them and then taking them back to join their team. The children who have been caught then become crows. If the leader calls 'cranes' the same process occurs with the cranes doing the chasing. Sometimes the leader may elongate the beginning of the word by starting with 'crrrrr . . . . . .' so the children are unsure which team is going to be named. This adds excitement to the game. Equally the leader may call out a word that begins with 'ccrrrr', such as, 'crickets', 'crocodiles' or 'crabs' to confuse the children and add to the excitement. The team who captures all the members of the opposite team wins.

Detective game: One child is chosen to be the detective and leaves the room. Another child is chosen to be the thief and given a piece of jewellery to hide in a pocket of another child in the group. The children must look carefully at the thief so they can remember what she or he looks like and can describe her/him. The detective is brought into the room and asks questions of all the children in the group to determine the identity of the thief. They must be able to answer the detective's questions correctly but without giving away the identity of the thief by looking at him. The questions the detective asks must be ones that can be answered by 'yes' or 'no'. For example, 'has the thief got black hair?' or 'is the thief wearing jeans?' The detective must listen carefully to each clue and look carefully at each child to match the clues in order to identify the thief.

Draw a feeling: Invite each child to draw, using felt pens, coloured lines, shapes or objects to illustrate how they feel right now. Invite other children to guess from the drawings how each child is feeling.

Expressing your feelings: The group is divided into two teams A and B. Each team is given an equal number of tokens. Each child chooses a card from the feeling box. On each card is written a word to describe a feeling, such as happy, excited, scared, terrified, surprised, mad, upset, embarrassed, disappointed, bored, proud, sad, annoyed, worried, etc. Team A then lines up and one at a time mimes the feelings on their cards. Team B has to guess what these are. For every correct guess, team B receives a token from team A. This process is repeated with team B miming. At the end, each team counts the number of tokens they have and distributes them evenly among their group. These tokens can then be included in the final tally for each child.

Expressing feelings – social skills role plays:

1. With hands on hips and overpowering stance say, 'I'd love it if you went and found my text book and gave it back to me, Jenny'.
2. Looking puzzled, rubbing the side of your face, say, 'Yes I understand everything that you are telling me. I'll go and do it right now.'
3. With your hands clasped tightly behind the back, and your eyes wide open, say, 'I'd love to go on the roller coaster with you.'
4. With your arms folded tightly across chest, say, 'Yes I'm really sorry.'

Find the dinosaur: Before the group begins two different dinosaurs are drawn on large separate pieces of paper. The pictures are then each cut up into eight pieces to produce two jigsaw puzzles. The puzzle pieces are identified on the back with a coloured dot, red for one dinosaur and blue for the other. The pieces are hidden around the room for the children to find and put together. The children are divided into two teams, one to find the pieces of puzzle marked with a red dot, and the other to find the pieces of puzzle marked with a blue dot. Once a puzzle is put together, the children are told to search for a toy dinosaur, which is also hidden in the room and looks like the puzzle picture. The first team to find their toy dinosaur wins.

Feeling small: Each child is given a small piece of clay or modelling dough to make a sculpture of 'feeling small' or 'being left out'. Discussion follows to help the children realise that these feelings of 'feeling small' and 'being left out' can change. With additional clay they can change their sculptures to be representationally more positive and powerful.

Fix my spaceship: This is a memory game where several objects are placed in full view of the group. The objects are covered after three minutes. Each group then cooperates as a team to write down as many objects as they can remember.

Fun box: Arrange four to six objects in a box. Let the children inspect and name the objects in the box. Warn them that you will move the items around and that they will then have to put them back in the same arrangement. Ask the children to close their eyes and then move some of the objects. Tell the children to open their eyes, tell you what objects have been moved and put them back where they were.

Guess what is happening: Choose any picture from a magazine, remove any words or captions that might indicate what is happening. Invite each child to put their own words to the picture to explain what they believe is happening in the picture.

Hoops: This activity is good as a joining exercise. Place several hoops on the ground. Inside each hoop place a large name tag with a child's name written on it. Invite the children to each find their name and sit inside the relevant hoop. Talk about the hoop being their 'space' and this being a space which they own. Use the hoops later as a contained area for time-outs if necessary. Invite each child to call out their name and share one thing they can do inside their space, for example, kneel, stand, curl up, read, listen to tapes.

Hotspots: This activity is useful when processing issues regarding trust and for encouraging confidence in the ability of others. Each child chooses a partner. One partner is blindfolded while the other stands at the opposite end of the room. A number of large paper plates are then scattered around the floor to create hotspots. The partner who can see then helps the blindfolded partner to move from one side of the room to the other without treading on the hotspots by giving instructions such as 'take two steps sideways, to your left'. The object is to help the blindfolded partner move from one end of the room to the other without treading on a paper plate by using only verbal instructions.

Human tunnel ball: Two teams line up with their legs astride. At a signal the first player in each team crawls through the legs of his/her team to stand at the back. The first team to finish crouches down on the floor.

I think, I feel, I want: The children are invited to find partners and sit facing their partners. They are then instructed to talk to their partners starting each sentence with 'I think' or 'I feel' or 'I want'. They are then invited to share with their partners how it feels to talk when starting each sentence with 'I'. The leader may ask questions such as 'what happened?', 'did you learn anything new about your partner?', 'did you discover anything new about yourself?' and 'what kinds of things did you learn?'.

Iceberg Activity: Each child is given a marble and a flat piece of expanded polystyrene which has been cut into a shape. The marble is then inserted into one edge of the expanded polystyrene. The shapes are next floated in buckets of water. The marble ends will sink. The children are encouraged to write words describing negative feelings on the parts of the expanded polystyrene shapes which sink and positive feelings on the parts of the expanded polystyrene shapes which stay above the water line. Attention is drawn to the fact that when the expanded polystyrene 'iceberg' is pushed over, negative feelings appear above the water line. This can be used as a metaphor for polarities within self.

It's not always happy at my house: Video tape produced by Kids Rights, 10100 Park Cedar Drive, Charlotte, NC 28210 USA.

Joining or rejoining: This activity helps the children learn and remember each other's names. The children are invited to sit in a circle on cushions they have chosen. The leader then calls out a child's name and throws a cushion to that child. The child receiving the cushion looks around the group and repeats the activity, calling out a child's name and then throwing the cushion to that child. Thus the cushion goes from child to child with each child calling out the name of the child who is to catch the cushion. The leader then invites the children to continue the activity with several cushions being used at the same time. The resulting mayhem can be fun.

Make a clay shape: The children are invited to make a clay shape that will let others know how they feel 'right now'. They can then be invited to combine their shapes with other shapes made by children who feel the same as they do. Some children may prefer to stay alone with their own shape and feeling. The children can then be invited to change their shapes to express other feelings. The concept of feelings and changing feelings can be discussed.

Make me laugh: Working in pairs, one child in each pair has two minutes to do anything they can to make their partner laugh without touching them. The children are then invited to swap roles. The whole group then discusses issues related to provocation.

Man the lifeboat: Draw a chalk line down the centre of the room or stick a long piece of masking tape to the floor to represent the lifeboat. Players stand in the middle of the room on one side of the line. The leader gives the following commands in any order:

- 'Man the lifeboat'. When this command is given players must move to the other side of the line.
- 'Abandon ship'. When this command is given players must fling themselves on the floor on their backs.
- 'Sharks'. When this command is given players must lie face down on the floor.
- 'Captain Aboard'. When this command is given players must stand, salute and say, 'Aye, aye, sir'.

The leader can call these commands out in any order and at an ever increasing pace. After each command, the last player to obey drops out and watches this amusing game.

Mouse and cheese poster: Draw a piece of cheese on the right hand side of the page. Stick a strip of velcro to the poster in a horizontal line from the cheese stretching across to the far left hand side of the page. Draw a small mouse on a piece of cardboard with velcro stuck on the reverse side. The mouse can then be moved along the velcro line as solutions to hypothetical situations enable the mouse to get closer to its goal (the cheese).

219

Name steps: Players line up at one end of the room. The leader stands at the finish line and calls out letters. A player can move four steps forward whenever a letter is called out that is a capital letter in any of his or her names (first, middle or last). If a letter which is called out is a lower case letter from a player's names, two steps are allowed. The first person to reach the finish line takes the leader's place as the next caller.

Newspaper hockey: The group is divided into two equal teams. Two 'bats' are made by rolling up newspaper. The teams line up facing each other and about three metres apart. A screwed up newspaper 'ball' is placed in the centre, at an equal distance from each team. Team one numbers off, one, two, three, etc., starting from one end. Team two numbers off similarly but beginning from the opposite end from team one. Consequently, the number one child in team one will now be facing the child in team two who has the highest number. The leader places the two newspaper 'bats' on either side of the newspaper 'ball'. The leader then calls out a number. The children with that number race to the centre, pick up a bat and hit the newspaper ball to a designated goal at the end of the room, while their opponent attempts to hit the newspaper ball to their team's designated goal at the other end of the room. The team with the most number of goals wins.

Obstacle course: Hoops and sticks are laid out in a circle in alternating patterns. For example, two hoops, three sticks, two hoops, two sticks, one hoop, four sticks and so on. The leader calls out instructions, for example, jump in the hoops and walk between the sticks. Each child follows the leader around the group, following the instructions set down by the leader. This activity is a motor activity which is useful for expending energy yet also encourages turn taking and memory.

Paper chain: Get each child to make a paper chain of five links, so that each link can be used to represent one of five activities to be used in the group session. Ask the children to hang the chain by the first link from a nearby chair. As each activity finishes, the children are to cut off the bottom chain link to signal the end of that activity. This signals the end of one activity and gives permission to move to the next. This exercise is useful in helping children cope with transitions from one activity to another.

Partners: Ask the children to form pairs. Each pair is given a large sheet of poster paper ruled up into six squares and twelve objects. The twelve objects form sets of pairs; for example, a pencil and pencil sharpener, a ring and ring box, a stamp and envelope, a doll's cup and saucer, etc. The children sort the objects into associated pairs and place them on the poster paper so that each square contains a pair of associated objects. They then mix up the items and put them into a pair of socks. Each pair of children pass their socks to the next pair of children and the sorting process is repeated.

Pass the ball: The children sit in a circle. A large beach ball is used to throw from child to child in the group. When the ball is thrown to a child, that child has to call out his or her name and an adjective to describe how he or she is feeling. This is useful as a check-in activity.

Pass the trash: Divide the group into two teams. Draw a circle two metres in diameter on the floor, using chalk or masking tape. Put a large rubbish bin in the middle. Team one lies down around the bin with their heads against it. Give each team member a bat made of rolled up sheets of newspaper. Team two stands around the circle and is given balls of newspaper. Team two attempts to throw the paper balls into the bin. Team one tries to prevent the balls from going into the bin by batting the balls away with their bats. After an allocated time, play is halted and the leader then counts the balls in the can. Teams then switch positions and the game is played again.

Personal boundaries: Each child is given a large sheet of poster paper on which a series of concentric circles is drawn. In order of size the circles represent the following:

● The central circle represents the child's own personal space.
● Circle 2 represents a space where the child might engage in some physical contact such as hugging. Relatives and friends might be invited into this circle.
● Circle 3 is the good friend circle. This circle is for people where there are warm positive feelings. Personal information may be shared with people who come into this circle.
● Circle 4 is the 'okay people circle'. This circle includes people who are in the child's social system but are not close friends.
● Circle 5 is the 'other people circle'. It includes people who the child might meet but who don't belong within the smaller circles.
● Outside the outer circle is the space occupied by strangers.

When using the personal boundaries circles, the child is invited to describe the kinds of people who might be invited into each circle and explore behaviours that are connected with the invitation or rejection of people into those circles. Emphasis is placed on the child being in control of whether people move into particular circles or whether they are not allowed in.

Personal ID card: Personal ID cards, as shown in Appendix B, are useful for children who come from families where there is or has been violence (Peled and Davis, 1992). Polaroid photographs are taken of each child. They are trimmed and used in helping the children make personal identification cards. The children are encouraged to write safety plan information on their cards, including phone numbers which might be useful in an emergency, such as the police or the phone number of a supportive relative or neighbour.

Pick a face: The children sit in a circle. Several cards showing sketches of faces with different expressions on them are placed in the centre of a circle. The children are each invited to choose a card which best represents how he or she is feeling. Children in the group are asked to look at the expression on the face drawn on the card that a child has chosen and to guess how that child is feeling. The child concerned can then comment on the guesses. The process is repeated for each child in the group.

Pick a pillow: Invite the children to each choose a cushion (pillow) to represent how they are feeling, from a pile of coloured cushions of various sizes, shapes and designs. Once they have chosen cushions, ask them to sit in a circle. The group is then encouraged to guess how individual children are feeling emotionally (for example, sad, worried or excited) by looking at their cushions. For example, the leader might say, 'When you look at the cushion Nigel has chosen, can you guess how he is feeling?' Nigel can then be asked to confirm or amend the group's suggestions.

Pretty picture collage: Create a complex collage by cutting out and mounting a number of pictures on a large sheet of card. Show the collage to the children and ask them to name three items they see in the collage. These items will be numbered one, two and three. Turn the collage face down and hold up a card with a number on it, either '1' '2' or '3'. Ask the children to name the item that matches the number on the card. Repeat the activity using the same collage for several days in succession, but identifying different items in the picture and increasing the number of items to be remembered. Observe whether the children improve with repetition.

Problem solving (social skills role plays): The children are invited to role play the following scenarios:

1. You've made plans with two friends. While you are getting ready to meet them, another friend comes along and asks if she can join you. You don't want to include her. What can you say?
2. You see someone cheating on a test. What would you do if, (a) it is someone you like, and (b) it is someone you dislike?
3. While arguing on the telephone with a close friend, she becomes angry and hangs up on you. What would you do?
4. While talking with a friend, you remember that she borrowed money from you two weeks ago with a promise to repay it the next day. She has not paid you back yet. What would you do?
5. You're in charge of a group project for a social studies class exercise that is due to be submitted next week. All of the students in your group have worked hard except for one. What would you say to her or him?

Red balloon game: Each child is given a red balloon to blow up and is invited to imagine the balloon contains his or her anger. Sitting in a circle, the children are invited to share with the group how they can deal with their anger using their balloon. For example they may:

1. Keep blowing up the balloon until it bursts.
2. Let the air out slowly, either quietly, or with a noise.
3. Tie up the neck of the balloon so that it stays inflated.
4. Sit on the balloon until it explodes.

Use the balloon activity as a metaphor to discuss anger management.

Reporter: Three children are chosen as reporters from various newspapers. They are instructed to wait outside the room until called. The remaining children are shown an interesting picture and asked to describe what is happening in the picture. From these impressions, a story is created. One child is elected to be an eye witness. The picture is now removed, a reporter is called in, and the eyewitness tells the story. The second reporter is called in and told the story by the first reporter. Similarly the third reporter is called in and told the story by the second reporter. The final version is usually quite different from the original. The reporters are finally shown the picture to discuss the differences. The aim of the game is to demonstrate how messages become distorted and misunderstood if people are not listening and looking carefully.

Rewarding yourself (social skills role play): The children are invited to role play the following scenarios:

223

1. You have just been told that you have been nominated for school captain along with ten other children. How do you share this information with (a) your family, and (b) your friends?
2. You have just come tenth out of fifteen in a marathon race which was very demanding and gruelling. Although for some this may not seem to be very successful, for you it is a great achievement. How do you tell (a) your family, and (b) your friends?
3. This is the fifth time that you have received an award for coming top of the class in weekly spelling bees. How do you tell (a) your family, and (b) your friends?
4. You have been to the dentist for some dental work which has in the past been very painful. This time you were able to sit in the dentist's chair without responding in negative ways to the procedures. How do you tell (a) your family, and (b) your friends?

Ring thing: Choose five different rings (these can often be found in novelty shops). The leader puts a ring on each finger. Show the children in the group and tell them to remember which finger each ring is on. Remove all the rings and then invite the children to put the rings on one of their own hands, so that each ring is on the correct finger. This activity is useful for teaching visual memory skills.

Roll the ball: This activity is useful in helping children to understand turn-taking behaviour. The children sit in a circle. They are invited to complete a picture of a beetle by taking turns. When a tennis ball is rolled to a child in the circle, that child draws one part of a beetle on the whiteboard. The child returns to his or her place in the group and rolls the ball to someone else, and the process continues until the picture is complete.

Round Robin activity: Set up a number work stations involving activities such as bubble blowing, icing a biscuit, reading books, doing puzzles, using craft materials, etc. (there need to be at least as many stations as there are children in the group). Number these work stations 1,2,3. . . . Give each child a sheet of paper and divide it into sections. Ask the children to write down the numbers of the work stations to be completed, with the numbers being in the order in which they intend to work, so that each number is in a separate section of their sheet of paper. The children are then told to tick off the relevant numbers as they complete the activities at the various work stations. This activity is useful for helping children organise their own activity programme and to follow through by carrying it out.

Safety plan hand: The children are invited to trace around their hands and write activities they might do to keep themselves safe on each finger of the tracing.

Sardines: One child is selected to hide. The rest of the group is then invited to find the missing child. When the missing child is found, instead of exposing the child and the child's hiding space, the finder joins the missing child. Eventually all the children will end up in the same hiding place. This activity encourages joining, closeness and a sense of belonging.

Say 'no' check list: This check list is for use by children while observing a role play of a child who is resisting peer pressure by saying 'no'.

1. Face the person and make eye contact.
2. Stay calm and try to be friendly.
3. Say 'no' and give a reason.
4. Suggest something else to do.
5. Use the broken record technique. That is, calmly repeat your point.
6. Leave if the person persists.
7. Use positive self talk afterwards. For example, you might say to yourself, 'Well done, you did a good job'.

Secrets: The children are all issued with an identical piece of card and pencils. They are asked to write on the card a brief description of an abusive act they committed. The cards are then placed in a hat or box and mixed up. Each child is invited to select, at random, a card from the hat. Members in the group then read out what is written on the cards they have picked, and comment on the behaviours described in terms of abuse, circumstances, provocation, severity, etc. This activity allows for self-disclosure in a non-threatening way.

Self-management (social skills role play): The children are encouraged to role-play the following scenarios:

1. A friend gives you a gift that you don't like or want. How do you respond?
2. Friends begin to sing 'happy birthday' to you in a public place. How do you react to this embarrassing situation?
3. A teacher often teases you in a joking way. This is really beginning to annoy you. What do you do?
4. A friend of yours shows you a new dress (or joggers) that was just purchased for a very special occasion and asks you for your

opinion. You think it is in very poor taste or not very nice. What do you say?

Self-portrait: This activity can be used with children to identify their own special characteristics. The children are invited to draw self-portraits and to make one thing about them look really different to how they really are. For example, to put glasses on the face, to draw their hair in a different style, or to draw themselves very tall or very short. The drawings can then be used to talk about similarities, differences, strengths and limitations.

Simon Says: One child stands out in front of the rest of the children and gives instructions, some of which are preceded by the words 'Simon says' and some of which are not. For example, 'Simon says put your hands on your hips', 'Simon says clap your hands', 'Put your hands on your head', etc. The children are to follow only those instructions which start with the words 'Simon says'. When a child makes a mistake and either fails to follow an instruction starting with 'Simon says' or starts to follow an instruction which did not begin with 'Simon says', that child is asked to drop out of the game. The last person left in the game is the winner.

Snap: This game is available commercially and is useful for encouraging turn-taking.

Sock puppets: Each child is invited to make a sock puppet to represent either a mouse or a monster. When the children have made their puppets the leader asks for a volunteer to play mother or father. A wig or a hat can be used to help establish the child in this role. The leader then asks a child with a mouse puppet to make a request to a parent, in a mouse-like way. A child with a the monster puppet then does the same, using a monster voice. The children are invited to talk about the differences between the ways in which the mouse and monster made their requests and asked to say whether the parent would be likely to grant the requests. The children are then invited to use a wizard puppet, already made by the leader, to make the same request in an appropriate way. This exercise is useful in helping children to use adaptive ways of asking to have their needs met.

Space encounter: The children are split into two groups (astronauts and aliens) to use a code (refer to 'coded messages' work-sheet) to write down three things they would like to communicate about themselves as a group, to the other group. For example, astronauts might say, 'We have travelled far – we are friendly – we like to have fun'. The messages are swapped and decoded by the other group.

Spotto: One player stands alone some distance from the other players and with his/her back to them. The other players then quietly attempt to sneak up on the player with his/her back turned. At various intervals this player turns around and calls 'Spotto' if he/she sees anyone moving. A person caught moving has to go back to the start line.

Stepping stones: Teams line up at opposite ends of the room to have a relay race. The players must cross the room by stepping only on two pieces of paper which must be alternately moved to provide stepping stones. Sometimes garden pots may be used instead of paper provided that the children are robust enough not to hurt themselves.

Sticker: Each child is given a number of sticky labels, one for every other member of the group, with different messages on them such as 'You make a great friend', 'You know lots of interesting things', 'You ask really good questions', 'You can think really well', 'You are fun to be around', 'I like the way you join in', 'You are a good listener', 'I'm glad you are here', 'You are an important person', 'You are great', 'You have a great smile', 'You know how to have fun', 'You have lots of energy' and 'You are so creative'. Some labels may simply have a happy face on them. Each child is invited to give the stickers to the children who they think match the comments on the stickers.

Take me back: This is an adaptation of the game 'crows and cranes'. One team is called, 'Martians' and the other team is called 'Marstronauts'. Children can be tricked by introducing confusing words such as 'marshmallows'.

Tape checklist: This activity is useful for children with ADHD. Make an audio- tape listing difficulties described by children with ADHD. For example, 'I have trouble organising myself', 'I have trouble relaxing', 'When I play with other kids, I find the rules confusing', etc. Give each child ten tokens. Play the tape, and every time the children hear a problem which they experience themselves, they are to throw a token into a hoop lying on the floor in the centre of the group.

Telephone role play: Two toy or old telephone receivers are used. Each child is invited to role play calling an emergency telephone number to report an incident which is life-threatening or frightening. This exercise can also be used to role play telephone calls to telephone help-lines where counselling services are available.

Television reporter: This activity helps children use visualisation as a way of improving organisational skills. The leader pretends to be a television reporter and tape records an interview with each child. The children are then asked about their plans for the session and about the

227

activities they plan to do that day. Encourage them to estimate how long the activities they plan will take and to plan the order in which they will do them. Ask questions such as 'what are you going to do first?', 'then what will you do?', 'What will you do after you play with the cat?', etc.

Thermometer: Each child has a work-sheet on which is drawn a picture of a thermometer. The grades on the thermometer begin at zero and go up to 100 in intervals of one. The thermometers are used to record the number of tokens each child receives as the group sessions proceed. The thermometers are collected at the end of each group and handed back at the beginning of each new session.

Thinking skills: Ask the children to put on brightly coloured hats and to call them, 'thinking caps'. The group leader starts by saying 'I have my thinking cap on, it's time for headwork. Put your thinking caps on'. The goal is to teach the children to listen, problem solve and think logically by asking questions. Begin with very concrete and easy questions. As the children's skills increase, progress to more complex questions. Some questions might focus on auditory comprehension for example, 'show me your favourite colour', 'How old are you', 'put your hand on your head', 'show me how to hop', 'point to Jason' (a child in the room).

Timer activity: A child is chosen to be the timer. The rest of the group are encouraged to engage in play activities located in different stations around the room (bubble blowing, icing a biscuit, reading a book, doing puzzles, working with craft materials, etc). The child chosen as timer is given a three minute egg timer. The first time the timer sounds gives a signal to the children that play at the current station is coming to an end. The second time the timer sounds all children move in a clockwise direction to the next play station. This activity is useful in helping children to work within time limits and prepares them for transitions to new activities. After completing several activities the children may be more able to judge temporal space and to estimate the amount of work that can be completed in that space.

Tweedledee and Tweedledum: Two teams face each other, but with some distance between them. They make eye contact. The first team player advances one step, looking the opposing player in the eye and saying, 'Tweedle Dee'. The opposing player then advances one step in a similar fashion, and says, 'Tweedle Dum'. This continues with players being instructed to try not to laugh until both players meet. Other team members follow suit. This game is helpful in discussing issues of provocation.

Weather chart: This is a check-in activity. A large rectangular sheet of card is divided into four quarters with a picture drawn in each quarter. The pictures depict various weather situations. For example, the four pictures might be of the sun, rain, windy weather and a quiet lake scene. A moveable pointer in the shape of an arrow is pinned to the centre of the card so it can be moved to point to any of the four pictures. The children are then each, in turn, asked to match the way they are feeling with a particular weather picture and to turn the pointer to the relevant picture. Other children in the group are then asked to guess how the child concerned might be feeling, based on the choice of the weather type.

What hands can do: Each child is invited to draw two pictures of how hands can help and how hands can hurt. The children are then invited to place their drawings on a long piece of poster paper stretched out on the floor. Next, they form pairs. One child in each pair dips their left hand into green paint and the other child dips their right hand into red paint. Each child then wanders along the poster paper deciding which pictures are helping hands and which are hurting hands. If a pair decide a picture represents a helping situation, the child in the pair with the green paint stamps their hand under the picture. If they decide the drawing represents a way in which hands can hurt, the child with the red paint stamps their hand under the picture. Before starting this exercise leaders must check to ensure participating children are not allergic or sensitive to the paint being used.

Word finding/verbal fluency activity: To help improve word finding and verbal fluency the leader asks questions such as, 'name two animals', 'name two kinds of food you like', 'name two things we write with', 'name two kinds of pet', 'name two things we use on our hair', 'how many noses do you have?', 'how do you know when a dog is angry?', 'would you like to fly up to the moon?', 'name all the people who help us', 'name all the things we can eat for breakfast', 'name all the sounds you hear at the zoo', etc.

Appendix B: Work-sheets

The work-sheets included in this appendix are suitable for use in group work with children. Readers are welcome to photocopy them for their own personal use when working with children in groups. The work-sheets are copyright, and must not be used for other purposes. We find they are easiest to use if they are enlarged to A4 size. The list below gives the page number for each work-sheet.

ALL ABOUT ME !

Your ADHD is only one part of you. There are many things about you that make you special. Here is a chance to talk about yourself. When you fill in these sentences you will know that they describe you.

I am very good at
....

This year I have been better at
....

My favourite subject at school is
....

The subject I like least is
....

One of the best books that I ever read was..

If I could travel anywhere in the world I would like to go to ....

I like to ....when I play with a friend.

I like to...with my family.

My favourite meal is...

If I could plan the perfect day this is what I would want to do
in the morning ....
in the afternoon..
in the evening...

Something about myself that I would like to change is....................................

What I like best about myself is...

Chart Your Course.......

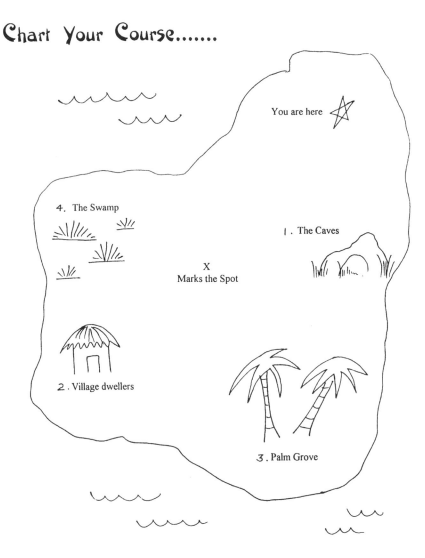

You are here

4. The Swamp

1. The Caves

X
Marks the Spot

2. Village dwellers

3. Palm Grove

CODES AND CODED MESSAGES.

Message 1
Go to the swamp

Message 2
Go to the village dwellers

Message 3
Go to the caves

Message 4
Go to the palm grove

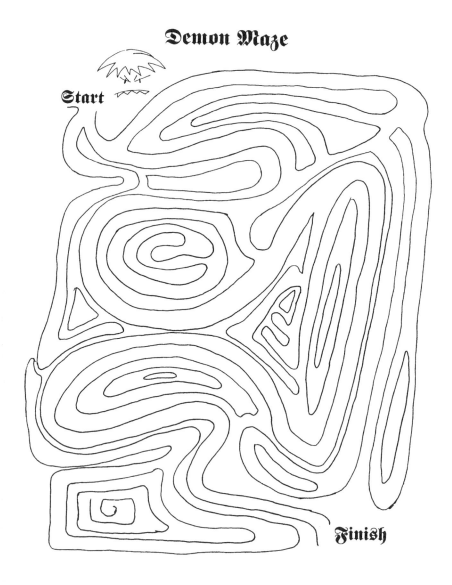

Demon Maze

Start

Finish

Fantasy Friend

If I Had the perfect friend they would be......

Male...........................
Female.......................
Hair colour..................
Colour of eyes.............
Would like games such as...
Would like to go to places such as...
Would have interests such as..
Would believe in things such as..
Would value, and see as important, things like.............................

He/she would be able to give me...
I would be able to give them...
I would need them to have qualities like ....

Have you ever had a friend like this?..
Do you know anybody like your fantasy friend?............................
How would you go about finding a friend like this?.......................

Forest Creatures

THE GAME BOARD

FINISH	Jump for joy	Sing Old McDonald, include duck, cow and sheep	Home Stretch Stretch and Yawn for your partner
Use the craft materials available and make a card for your partner	Play one of these games before moving on (Connect - 4 or Dominoes)	Fill out the work-sheet "Reward Yourself" and tell your partner about one of the situations that you feel proud of.	Using the Monster mask ask (as a demanding monster) the King (your partner) if you can sleep overnight in the castle. The King says, "No!" Then use the Mouse mask (and ask as a timid mouse) The King still says, "No!" Now ask as yourself and see how the King responds. Move one space forward
Go back 4 spaces OR if that task has been done...... go back 1 space OR if that task has been done...... go forward one space			
Pick an animal from the pile of plastic miniatures and describe to your partner how you are like, and how you are not like that animal!	Go back 2 spaces OR If that task has been done...... Go forward one space	Go back 1 space OR If that task has been done...... move forward 2 spaces	
		Choose three cards from the pile and mime the word for your partner. Can they guess? (Bullying, sharing, lying, stealing etc)	
		Throw again	**START**

237

How do You Relax?

Because many children with ADHD find it difficult to sit still or stay focused for a long time other people will often tell them to SETTLE DOWN!!

Below is a list of ways to help some kids relax. Put a tick against the ones that you have tried that work for you. If you haven't tried to relax you might find that these ideas will work for you too.

You might want to think of some other ways in which to relax.

Breathe deeply and count to 20.................................

Exercise eg., jogging, bicycle riding, swimming...........

Soak in a bath, or take a long shower........................

Listen to quiet music in a private place....................

OR

....

....

....

Draw yourself relaxing:

"If i was................."

Imagine that you are blue!
Imagine that you are red!
Describe what it would be like. Which do you prefer?
Can you be any of those things now?
Try imagining that you are one of these...............

A sports car or a campervan

A jet or a small private aeroplane

A ocean or a lake

Prime Minister of your country or Captain of the school

A fireman or a policeman

A tree or a flower

An eagle or a hummingbird

A hammer or a nail

A cup or a saucer

An ant or a fly

The magic forest

Once upon a time there was a young child called Matilda. Matilda's parents were the king and queen of the magic forest. The king, Matilda's father was very . . . . and the queen, Matilda's mother was always . . . . Matilda was the kind of child who never . . . . but always . . . . Sometimes the king, the queen and Matilda would . . . . but they never . . . . All of them would sometimes go . . . . and Matilda would feel . . . . One day while walking in the magic forest, Matilda lost her way. She tried and tried to see if she could get back home to the castle. Matilda became . . . . After a while a wizard came hobbling along the path and told Matilda . . . . The wizard also gave Matilda . . . . The first thing that Matilda did was . . . . and she . . . . Finally, after wandering around for a long time, Matilda recognised the path back to the castle. She hurried towards it but suddenly she came across a . . . . Now she felt . . . . As the sun was setting Matilda finally trudged through the castle gates and into the castle where the king and queen were very, very . . . . Her father the king told Matilda . . . . Matilda felt . . . . so told the king and queen . . . . It had been a very tiring day for Matilda and she fell asleep. The king and queen watched Matilda as she slept and thought . . . . The next morning Matilda woke up and said to herself, "today . . . . "

Make a Frog

Materials needed: stiff card, scissors, a knife and board for scoring, paints, and an elastic band. Cut a rectangle of card 20 by 10 cm and round off the corners. Pierce a hole at either end of the card. Score the card across the middle, fold it and bend it backwards and forwards a few times. (figure 1)

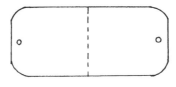

Fig. 1

Paint or draw an outstretched frog on the card (figure 2)

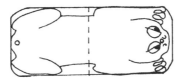

Fig. 2

Loop the elastic band through the hole at one end of the card and knot it through the hole at the other end (figure 3).

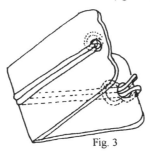

Fig. 3

Bend the card in two so that the elastic band is stretched and held taunt. Place it on the table and let go so that the frog jumps.

241

MY MUM & DAD SAY THINGS LIKE..........

```
┌─────────────────────────┐
│                         │
│                         │
│                         │
│                         │
│                         │
│                         │
│                         │
│                         │
└─────────────────────────┘
```

<u>Hop</u> into bed!
or
Have you left your manners at home?
or
Drink it <u>up</u>

What strange things does yours say?

_____
_____
_____
_____
_____
_____
_____
_____

PERSONAL PROTECTION ID CARD

Place photograph here	Personal protection plan
	•
	•
Name...............................	•
Address.............................	•
....	•
Phone...............................	•

Here is your very own ID card.

You can write the details of your protection plan on this card to remind you of the things you can do when you are not feeling safe.

Polarities

Underline the sentences that sound like you

I am friendly

I am a bully

I am loveable

I am lonely   I am dull

I am wanted

I am hated

I am a failure

I am fun

I am a winner

I am not OK

I am lively

I am successful

I have good ideas

I can make good decisions

I can solve problems

I can ask questions

I am not a good listener

WHAT DO PEOPLE DO WITH THEIR FACES...........................

...............................TO SHOW HOW THEY ARE FEELING ?

REFERENCES

Achenbach, T.M. and Edelbrock, C. (1991) *Child Behavior Checklist and Related Materials* (Burlington, Vermont: University of Vermont).

Adelman, H. and Taylor, L. (1982) Enhancing the motivation and skills needed to overcome interpersonal problems. *Learning Disability Quarterly*, **5**: 438–46.

Akin, T., Cowan, D., Dunne, G., Palomares, S., Schilling, D. and Shuster, S. (1990) *The Best Self-esteem Activities: for the Elementary Grades* (Spring Valley, CA: Innerchoice Publishing).

Andersen, T. (1991) Guidelines for practice. In T. Andersen (ed) *The Reflecting Team: Dialogues and Dialogues about the Dialogues* (New York: Norton).

Andersson, B. (1989) Effects of public day-care: a longitudinal study. *Child Development*, **60**: 857–66.

Andersson, B. (1992) Effects of day-care on cognitive and socioemotional competence of thirteen-year-old Swedish school children. *Child Development*, **63**: 20–36.

Bandura, A. (1971) *Social learning theory* (New York: General Learning Press).

Bandura, A. (1986) *Social Foundations of Thought and Action: a Social Cognitive Theory* (Englewood Cliffs, NJ: Prentice Hall).

Barry, J. and von-Baeyer, C. (1997) Brief cognitive behavioural group treatment for children's headache. *Clinical Journal of Pain*, **13**: 215–20.

Beck, A.T. (1993) Cognitive Therapy: past, present and future. *Journal of Consulting and Clinical Psychology*, **61**(2): 194–8.

Belsky, J. (1988) The effects of infant day-care reconsidered. *In*, **3**: 234–72.

Belsky, J. and Steinberg, L. (1982) The effects of day-care: a critical review. *Child development*, **49**: 929–49.

Bem, S.L. (1989) Genital knowledge and gender constancy in preschool children. *Child Development*, **60**: 649–62.

Berkovitz, I.H. (1987a) Application of group therapy in secondary schools. In F.J.C. Azima and L.H. Richmond (eds). *Adolescent Group Psychotherapy* (pp. 99–123) (Madison, CT: International Universities Press).

Berkovitz, I.H. (1987b) Value of group counselling in secondary schools. *Adolescent Psychiatry*, **14**: 522–45.

Berndt, T.J. (1997) *Child Development* (2nd ed) (Madison, WI: Brown and Benchmark).

Bertcher, H.J. and Maple, F. (1985) Elements and issues in group composition. In M. Sundel, P. Glaffer, R. Sarri and R. Vinter (eds) *Individual Change in Small Groups* (2nd ed, pp. 180–202) (New York: Free Press).

Bilides, D.G. (1990) Race, colour, ethnicity, and class: Issues of biculturalism in school-based adolescent counselling groups. *Social Work with Groups*, **13**: 43–58.

Bilides, D.G. (1992) Reaching inner-city children: A group work program model for a public middle school. *Social Work with Groups*, **15**: 129–44.

Bloch, S. (1986) Therapeutic factors in group psychotherapy. In A.J. Frances and R.E. Hales (eds) *Annual Review,* **5** (pp. 678–98) (Washington, DC: American Psychiatric Press).

Blonk, R.B., Prims, P.J., Sergeant, J.A., Ringrose, J. and Brinkman, A.G. (1996) Cognitive behavioural group therapy for socially incompetent children: Short-term and maintenance effects with a clinical sample. *Journal of Clinical Child Psychology,* **25**: 215–24.

Braungart, L.M., Plomin, R., DeFries, J.C. and Fulker, D.W. (1992) Genetic influence on tester-rated temperament as assessed by Bayleys Infant Behaviour Record: Nonadoptive and adopted siblings and twins. *Developmental Psychology,* **28**: 40–7.

Brown, T. (2000) *Brown Attention Deficit Disorder Scales – Children's Version* (San Antonio: The Psychological Corporation).

Bugental, J.F.T. (1978) *Psychotherapy and Process: the Fundamentals of an Existential–Humanistic Approach* (New York: Random House).

Campbell, S.B. (1990) *Behaviour problems in preschool children,* (New York: Guilford Press).

Carey, W.B. (1995) *Carey Temperament Scales* (Scotsdale: Behavioral–Developmental Initiatives).

Carr, W. and Kemmis, S. (1986) *Becoming Critical: Education, Knowledge and Action Research* (London: Falmer).

Clarkson, P. (1989) *Gestalt Counselling in Action,* (London: Sage).

Clarke-Stewart, K.A. (1988) Parents effects on children's development: a decade of progress? *Journal Of Applied Developmental Psychology,* **9**: 41–84.

Cohen, A.M. and Smith, R.D. (1976) *The Critical Incident in Growth Groups: Theory and Technique* (La Jolla: University Associates Inc).

Cole, D. and Kammer, P.P. (1984) Support groups for children with divorced parents. *Elementary School Guidance and Counselling,* **19**: 88–94.

Conners, C.K. (1997) *Conners' Rating Scales – Revised* (New York: Multi-Health Systems).

Coopersmith, S. (1981) *Coopersmith Self-Esteem Inventories* (Palo Alto, CA: Consulting Psychologists Press).

Corey, G. (1996) *Theory and Practice of Counseling and Psychotherapy* (Pacific Grove, CA: Books/Cole).

Cowen, E.L., Hightower, A.D., Pedro-Carroll, J. and Work, W.C. (1989) School-based models for primary preventional programming with children. *Prevention in Human Services,* **7**: 133–60.

deShazer, S. (1991) *Putting Difference to Work* (New York: Norton).

Dies, K.R. (1996) The unfolding of adolscent groups: a five-phase model of development. In P. Kymissis and D.A. Halperin (eds) *Group Therapy with Children and Adolescents* (Washington, DC: American Psychiatric Press Inc).

Dolgin, M.J., Summer, E., Zaidel, N. and Zaizov, R. (1997) A structured group intervention for siblings of children with cancer. *Journal of Child and Adolescent Group Therapy,* **7**: 3–18.

Downey, J. (1996) Psychological counselling of children and young people. In R. Woolfe and W. Dryden (eds) *Handbook of Counseling Psychology* (London: Sage).

Dryden, W. (1990) *Rational Emotive Counselling in Action* (London: Sage).

247

Dubow, E.R., Tisak, J., Causey, D., Hryshko, A. and Reid, G. (1991) Two-year longitudinal study of stressful life events, social support, and social problem-solving skills: Contributions to children's behavioural and academic adjustment. *Child Development*, **62**: 583–99.

Dwivedi, K.N. (1993a) Introduction. In K.N. Dwivedi (ed) *Group Work with Children and Adolescents* (London: Jessica Kingsley).

Dwivedi, K.N. (1993b) Conceptual frameworks. In K.N. Dwivedi (ed) *Group Work with Children and Adolescents* (London: Jessica Kingsley).

Ehly, S. and Dustin, R. (1989) *Individual and Group Counseling in Schools* (New York: Guilford).

Ellis, A. (1995) Rational Emotive Behavior Therapy. In R.J. Corsini and D. Wedding (eds) *Current Psychotherapies* (5th ed) (Itasca, IL: Peacock).

Farmer, S. and Galaris, D. (1993) Support groups for children from divorce. *American Journal of Family Therapy*, **21**: 40–50.

Fatout, M.F. (1996) *Children in Groups: a Social Work Perspective* (Westport, Connecticut: Auburn House).

Felner, R.D., Farber, F. and Primavera, J. (1983) Transitions and stressful life events: A model for primary prevention. In R.D. Thelma, L. Jason, J. Moritsugu and F. Farber (eds) *Prevention psychology: Theory, Research, and Practice* (Elmsford, NY: Pergamon).

Fiedler, F.E. (1967) *A Theory of Leadership Effectiveness* (New York: McGaw-Hill).

Frances, A., Clarkin, J.F. and Marachi, J.P. (1980) Selection criteria for outpatient group psychotherapy. *Hospital Community Psychiatry*, **31**: 245–50.

Freedman, D.G. (1969) Ethnic differences in babies. *Human Nature*, **2**: 36–43.

Frydenberg, E. and Lewis, R. (1993) *Adolescent Coping Scale* (Melbourne: ACER).

Gajewski, N. and Mayo, P. (1989) *Social Skills Strategies* (New York: Thinking Publications).

Geldard, K. and Geldard, D. (1997) *Counselling children – a practical introduction* (London: Sage).

Geldard, K. and Geldard, D. (1999) *Counselling adolescents – a pro-active approach* (London: Sage).

Gendlin, E.T. (1981) *Focusing* (2nd ed) (New York: Bantam).

George, R.L. and Dustin, D. (1988) *Group Counselling: Theory and Practice* (New Jersey: Prentice Hall).

Gilligan, C.S. (1986) Remapping development: the power of divergent data. In L. Cirillo and S. Wapner (eds) *Value Presuppositions in Theories of Human Development* (Hillsdale, NJ: Erlbaum).

Grayson, A.D. and Deluca, R.V. (1995) Group therapy for boys who have experienced sexual abuse: Is it the treatment of choice? *Journal of Child and Adolescent Group Therapy*, **5**(2): 57–82.

Gordon, B.N., Schroder, C.S. and Abrams, J.M. (1990) Children's knowledge of sexuality: age and social class differences. *Journal of Clinical Child Psychology*, **19**: 33–43.

Greenberg, L., Elliott, R. and Lietaer, G. (1994) Research on experiential psychotherapies. In A.E. Bergin and S. Garfield (eds) *Handbook of Psychotherapy and Behaviour Change* (New York: Wiley).

Gresham, F.M. and Elliott, S.M. (1990) *Social Skills Rating System* (Circle Pines, MN: American Guidance Service).

Gundersen, B.H., Melas, P.S. and Skar, J.E. (1981) Sexual behaviour of preschool children: Teachers observations. In L.L. Constantine and F.M. Martinson (eds) *Children and Sex: New Findings, New Perspectives* (Boston: Little, Brown).

Gupta, M.R., Hariton, J.R. and Kernberg, P.F. (1996) Diagnostic groups for school-age children: group behaviour and DSM-IV diagnosis. In P. Kymissis and D.A. Halperin (eds) *Group Therapy with Children and Adolescents* (Washington, DC: American Psychiatric Press Inc).

Harris, W.J. (1984) The making better choices program. *Pointer*, **29**: 16–19.

Harrison, P. and Oakland, T. (2000) *Adaptive Behavior Assessment System* (San Antonio: The Psychological Composition).

Hastings, A. (1999) Transpersonal Psychology: the fourth force. In D. Moss (ed) *Humanistic and Transpersonal Psychology: a Historical and Biographical Sourcebook*, (Westport, CT: Greenwood).

Henry, S. (1992) *Group Skills in Social Work* (2nd ed) (Pacific Grove, CA: Brooks/Cole).

Herndon, C.H. (1985) Stage V: Termination. In A.M. Siepker and C.S. Kandaras (eds) *Group Therapy with Children and Adolescents: a Treatment Manual* (New York: Human Sciences Press).

Hess, A.M., Rosenberg, N.S. and Levy, G.K. (1990) Reducing truancy in students with mild handicaps. *Remedial and Special Education*, **11**: 14–28.

Hoag, M.J. and Burlingame, G.M. (1997) Child and adolescent group psychotherapy: A narrative review of effectiveness and the case for meta analysis. *Journal of Child and Adolescent group therapy*, **7**: 51–68.

Hoffman, C.E. (1984) Group session in the middle school. *Children Today*, **13**: 25–6.

Hogan, R. and Emler, N. (1995) Personality and moral development. In W. Kurtines and J. Gewirtz *Moral development: an introduction* (Needham Heights, MA: Allyn & Bacon).

Hollander, E.P. (1985) Leadership and power. In G. Lindzey and E. Aronson (eds) *Handbook of Social Psychology*, vol. 2, 3rd ed (New York: Random House).

Howarth, E.R. and Riester, A.E. (1997) The efficacy of activity group therapy in a residential treatment centre. *Journal of Child and Adolescent Group Therapy*, **7**: 19–39.

Jaffe, P.G., Wolfe, D.A. and Wilson, S.K. (1990) *Children of battered women* (Beverly Hills, CA: Sage Publications).

Jaffe, S.L. and Kalman, B. (1991) Group therapy. In J.M. Weiner (ed) *Textbook of Child and Adolescent Psychiatry* (Washington, DC: American Psychiatric Press).

Janov, A. (1970) *The Primal Scream: Primal Therapy, the Cure for Neurosis* (New York: Dell).

Kandaras, C.S. (1985) Stage IV: Cohesion. In A.M. Siepker and C.S. Kandaras (eds) *Group Therapy with Children and Adolescents: a Treatment Manual* (New York: Human Sciences Press).

Kelly, G.A. (1955) *The Psychology of Personal Constructs* (New York: Norton).

King, C.A. and Kirschenbaum, D.S. (1992) *Helping Young Children Develop Social Skills* (Pacific Grove, CA: Brooks/Cole).

Kohlberg, L. (1984) *The psychology of moral development: Essays on Moral Development* (Vol 2) (San Francisco: Harper & Row).

Kopala, M. and Keitel, M.A. (1998) Groups for traumatic stress disorder. In K. Stoiber and T. Kratochwill (eds) *Handbook of Group Intervention for Children and Families* (pp. 236–67) (Boston, MA: Allyn & Bacon Inc).

Kovacs, M. (1992) *Children's Depression Inventory* (North Tonawanda: Multi-Health Systems Inc).

Kraft, I. (1996) 'History' In P. Kymissis and D.A. Halperin (eds) *Group Therapy with Children and Adolescents* (Washington, DC: American Psychiatric Press Inc).

Kurtines, W.M. and Gewirtz, J.L. (1995) *Moral Development: an Introduction* (Needham Heights: Allyn & Bacon).

Kymissis, P. (1996) Developmental approach to socialization and group formation. In P. Kymissis and D.A. Halperin (eds) *Group Therapy with Children and Adolescents* (Washington, DC: American Psychiatric Press Inc).

Kymissis, P. and Halperin, D.A. (eds) (1996) *Group Therapy with Children and Adolescents* (Washington, DC: American Psychiatric Press Inc).

Lampel, A.K. (1985) Stage II: Exploration. In A.M. Siepker and C.S. Kandaras (eds) *Group Therapy with Children and Adolescents: a Treatment Manual* (New York: Human Sciences Press).

LeCroy, C. and Rose, S.R. (1986) Helping children cope with stress. *Social Work in Education*, **9**: 5–15.

Levine, M.D., Gordon, B.N. and Reed, M.S. (1987) *Developmental Variation and Learning Disorders* (Cambridge, MA: Educators Publishing Service).

Lewin, K. (1951) Field Theory in Social Science. In D. Cartwright (ed) *Selected Theoretical Papers* (New York: Harper).

Lewin, K., Lippitt, R. and White, R.K. (1994) Patterns of Aggressive Behavior in Experimentally Created 'Social Climates', *Journal of Social Psychology*, **10**: 217–99.

Lewis, L.H. (1985) Stage III: Anxiety. In A.M. Siepker and C.S. Kandaras (eds) *Group Therapy with Children and Adolescents: a Treatment Manual* (New York: Human Sciences Press).

Lock, J. (1996) Developmental considerations in the treatment of school-age boys with ADHD: An example of a group treatment approach. *Journal of the American Academy of Adolescent Psychiatry*, **35**: 1557–9.

Lopez, J. (1991) Group work as a protective factor for immigrant youth. *Social Work with Groups*, **14**: 29–42.

Mahrer, A.R. (1983) *Experiential Psychotherapy: Basic Practices* (New York: Brunner/Mazel).

Malekoff, A. (1997) *Groupwork with Adolescents* (New York: Guilford).

McCormack, B. and Sinason, V. (1996) Mentally handicapped children and adolescents. In P. Kymissis and D.A. Halperin (eds) *Group Therapy with Children and Adolescents* (Washington, DC: American Psychiatric Press Inc).

Mercer, J.R. and Lewis, J.F. (1982) *Adaptive Behavior Inventory for Children* (San Antonio: The Psychological Corporation).

Moos, R.H. and Humphrey, B. (1986) *Group Environment Scale* (Palo Alto, CA: Consulting Psyhologists Press).

Naglieri, J.A., LeBuffe, P.A. and Pfeiffer, S.I. (1993) *Devereux Behaviour Rating Scale – School Form* (San Antonio: The Psychological Corporation).

Nash, H. (1994) *Kids, Family and Chaos: Living with Attention Deficit Disorder* (Torrensville, Australia: Ed-Med).

Neeper, R., Lahey, B.B. and Frick, P. (1990) *Comprehensive Behaviour Rating Scale* (San Antonio: The Psychological Corporation).

O'Rourke, K. and Worzbyt, J.C. (1996) *Support Groups for Children* (Washington, DC: Accelerated Development).

Owens, K. (1993) *The world of the child* (New York: Macmillan).

Patterson, S. (1990) *I wish the Hitting Would Stop: a Workbook for Children Living in Violent Homes* (Fargo, ND: Rape & Abuse Crisis Center).

Pedro-Carroll, J.L., Alpert-Gillis, L.J. and Cowen, E.L. (1992) An evaluation of the efficacy of a preventive intervention for fourth-sixth grade urban children of divorce. *The Journal of Primary Prevention*, 13: 115–30.

Peled, E. and Davis, D. (1992) Goupwork with Child Witnesses of Domestic Violence: a Practitioner's Manual (Minneaplis: Domestic Abuse Project).

Perls, F.S., Hefferline, R.F. and Goodman, P. (1951) *Gestalt Therapy* (New York: Julian Press).

Piaget, J. (1962) *Play, Dreams and Imitations* (New York: Norton).

Piaget, J. (1971) *Psychology and Epistomology: Towards a Theory of Knowledge* (Translated by Rosin, A.) (New York: Viking).

Pierce, R.A., Nichols, M.P. and DuBrin, J.R. (1983) *Emotional Expression in Psychotherapy* (New York: Gardner Press).

Piers, E.V. and Harris, D.B. (1984) *Piers–Harris Childrens Self Concept Scale* (CA: Western Psychological Services).

Plomin, R. (1989) Environment and genes: Determinants of behaviour. *American Psychologist*, 44: 105–11.

Posthuma, B.W. (1996) *Small Groups in Therapy Settings: Process and Leadership* (2nd ed) (Boston: Allyn & Bacon).

Rachman, A.W. and Raubolt, R. (1985) The clinical practice of group psychotherapy with adolescent substance abusers. In T.E. Bratter and C.G. Forrest (eds) *Alcoholism and Substance Abuse: Strategies for Clinical Intervention* (New York: Free Press).

Ray, L. (1994) *Raising the Roof: Issues and Opportunities Responding to Child Witnesses to Domestic Violence* (Holland Park, Qld: Talera Centre).

Reynolds, C.R. and Kamphaus, R.W. (1992) *Behavior Assessment System for Children* (Circle Pines, MN: American Guidance Service).

Reynolds, C.R. and Richmond, B.O. (1985) *Revised Childrens Manifest Anxiety Scale* (Los Angeles, CA: Western Psychological Services).

Rice, L.N. and Greenberg, L.S. (1992) Humanistic approaches to psychotherapy. In D. Freedheim (ed) *History of Psychotherapy: a Century of Change* (Washington, DC: American Psychological Association).

Richert, A.J. (1986) An experiential group treatment for behavioural disorders. *Techniques: A Journal for Remedial Education and Counselling*, 2: 249–55.

Rogers, C.R. (1955) *Client Centered Therapy* (Boston: Houghton-Mifflin).

Rogers, C.R. (1965) *Client Centered Therapy: its Current Practice, Implications, and Theory* (Boston: Houghton-Mifflin).

Rohde Jansen, A. (1957) *Sentence Completions* (New York: Ronald Press).

Romano, E., Grayston, A.D., Deluca, R.V. and Gillis, M.A. (1995) The thematic appercep- tion test as an outcome measure in the treatment of sexual abuse: Preliminary findings. *Journal of Child and Youth Care*, **10**: 37–50.

Rose, S. (1998) The role of research in group therapy with children and adolescents. In Stoiber, K.C. and Kratochwill, T.R. (eds) *Handbook of Group Intervention for Children and Families*, (pp. 47–67) (Boston, MA: Allyn & Bacon Inc).

Rose, S.D. (1998) *Group Therapy with Troubled Youth: A Cognitive Behavioural Interactive Approach* (California: Sage).

Rose, S.R. (1985) Development of children's social competence in classroom groups. *Social Work and Education*, **8**: 48–58.

Rose, S.R. (1986) Enhancing the social relationship skills of children: A comparative study of group approaches. *School Social Work Journal*, **10**: 76–85.

Rose, S.R. (1998) *Group Work with Children and Adolescents: Prevention and Intervention in School and Community Systems* (Beverly Hills: Sage).

Rose, S.D. and Edleson, J.L. (1987) *Working with Children and Adolescents in Groups: a Multi- method Approach* (San Francisco, CA: Jossey-Bass).

Rosenfeld, A., Bailey, R., Seigel, B. and Bailey, G. (1986) Determining incestuous contact between parent and child: frequency of children touching parents' genitals in a nonclinical population. *Journal of The American Academy of Child Psychiatry*, **25**: 481–4.

Santrock, J.W. (1996) *Child Development* (IA, USA: Brown and Benchmark).

Schnitzer de Neuhaus, M. (1985) Stage 1: Preparation. In A.M. Siepker and C.S. Kandaras (eds) *Group Therapy with Children and Adolescents: a Treatment Manual* (New York: Human Sciences Press).

Schroeder, C.S. and Gordon, B.N. (1991) *Assessment and Treatment of Childhood Problems: A Clinicians' Guide* (New York: Guilford Publications).

Shaw, M.E. (1981) *Group Dynamics: the Psychology of Small Group Behaviour* (3rd ed) (New York: McGraw-Hill).

Shelby, J. (1994) Psychological intervention with children in disaster relief shelters. *The Child, Youth, and Family Services Quarterly*, **17**: 14–18.

Siegal, M. and Storey, R. (1985) Day-care and children's conceptions of moral and social rules. *Child Development*, **56**: 1001–9.

Siepker, A.M. & Kandaras, C.S. (1985) *Group Therapy with Children and Adolescents: a Treatment Manual* (New York: Human Sciences Press).

Silveira, W.R. and Trafford, G. (1988) *Children Need Groups: a Practical Manual for Group Work with Young Children* (Aberdeen: Aberdeen University Press).

Snarey, J. (1995) In a communatarian voice: The sociological expansion of Kohlbergian theory, research, and practice. In W. Kurtines and J. Gewirtz (eds) *Moral Development: an Introduction* (Needham Heights: Allyn & Bacon).

Snarey, J. (1993) *How Fathers Care for the Next Generation* (Cambridge: Harvard Univer- sity Press).

Snarey, J. and Kelijo, K. (1991) In a Gemeinschaft voice: the cross-cultural expansion of moral development theory. *Handbook of Moral Behaviour and Development: Volume 1. Theory* (Hillsdale: Erlbaum).

Soo, E.S. (1996) Supervision. In P. Kymissis and D.A. Halperin (eds) *Group Therapy with Children and Adolescents* (Washington, DC: American Psychiatric Press Inc).

Speers, R.W. and Lansing, C. (1965) *Group Therapy in Childhood Psychoses* (Chapel Hill, NC: University of North Carolina Press).

Spitz, H.I. (1987) Cocaine abuse: therapeutic approaches. In H.I. Sptiz and J.S. Rosecan (eds) *Cocaine Abuse: New Directions in Treatment and Research* (New York: Brunner/Mazel).

Stark, K.D., Rouse, L.W. and Livingstone, R. (1991) Treatment of depression during childhood and adolescence: Cognitive-behavioural procedures for the individual and the family. In P.C. Kendall (ed) *Child and Adolescent Therapy; Cognitive-behavioural Approaches* (pp. 165–98) (New York: Guilford).

Swanson, A.J. (1996) Children in groups: indications and contexts. In P. Kymissis and D.A. Halperin (eds) *Group Therapy with Children and Adolescents* (Washington, DC: American Psychiatric Press Inc).

Teri, L. and Lewinsohn, P.M. (1985) Group intervention for unipolar depression. *Behaviour Therapist*, **8**: 109–11.

Tonkins, S. and Lambert, M.J. (1996) A treatment outcome study of bereavement groups for children. *Child and Adolescent Social Work Journal*, **13**: 3–21.

Toseland, R.W. and Siporin, M. (1986) When to recommend group treatment: A review of the clinical and the research literature. *International Journal of Group Psychotherapy*, **36**: 191–206.

Trounson, C.D. (1996) From chaos to cohesion: Group therapy with preschool-aged children. *Journal of Child and Adolescent Group Therapy*, **6**: 3–25.

Tuckman, B.W. and Jensen, M.A.C. (1977) Stages in small group development revisited, *Group and Organisational Studies*, **2**: 419–27.

Tuckman, J.P. (1995) Short term groups with children: The Yellow Brick Road to Healthy Development. *Journal of Child and Adolescent Group Therapy*, **5**: 3–17.

Varma, V. (1997) *Violence in Children and Adolescence* (London: Jessica Kingsley).

Vlietstra, A. (1982) Children's responses to talk instructions: page changes and training efforts. *Child Development*, **53**: 534–42.

Vogel, J. and Vernberg, E.M. (1993) Children's psychological responses to disaster. *Journal of Clinical Child Psychology*, **22**: 464–84.

Waas, G.A. and Graczyk, P.A. (1998) Group interventions for the peer rejective child. In K.C. Stoiber and T.R. Kratochwill (eds) *Handbook of Group Intervention for Children and Families* (pp. 141–158) (Boston, MA: Allyn & Bacon, Inc).

Walker, L.J. (1989) A longitudinal study of moral reasoning. *Child Development*, **60**: 157–66.

Wallace, I. (1996) *You and your ADD child* (Sydney, Australia: HarperCollins).

Walz, G.R. (1992) *Helping Students Cope with Crisis* (Michigan: Eric/Ann Arbor).

Waterman, J. (1986) Developmental considerations. In K. McFarlane and J. Waterman (eds) *Sexual Abuse of Young Children: Evaluation and Treatment* (New York: Guilford Press).

Watson, H.J., Vallee, J.M. and Mulford, W.R. (1981) *Structured Experiences and Group Development* (Canberra: Curriculum Development Centre).

Wheelan, S.A. (1994) *Group Processes: a Developmental Perspective* (Needham Heights, MA: Allyn & Bacon).

White, M. and Epston, D. (1990) *Narrative Means to Therapeutic Ends* (New York: Norton).

Yalom, I.D. (1980) *Existential Psychotherapy* (New York: Basic Books).

Index